The Christian Horseman's Companion

Other Books by Tom Moates:

Discovering Natural Horsemanship
Round-Up: A Gathering of Equine Writings
Six Colts, Two Weeks, Volume One
Six Colts, Two Weeks, Volume Two
Considering Horsemanship

The Honest Horsemanship Series:
A Horse's Thought
Between the Reins
Further Along the Trail
Going Somewhere
Passing It On

The Christian Horseman's Companion

Tom Moates

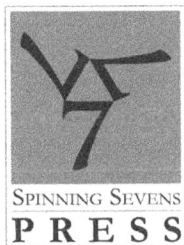

SPINNING SEVENS
PRESS

ISBN: 978-0-9992465-3-5

Cover design by Tom Moates and Emily Kitching.
Cover photo by Carol Moates.

Contents

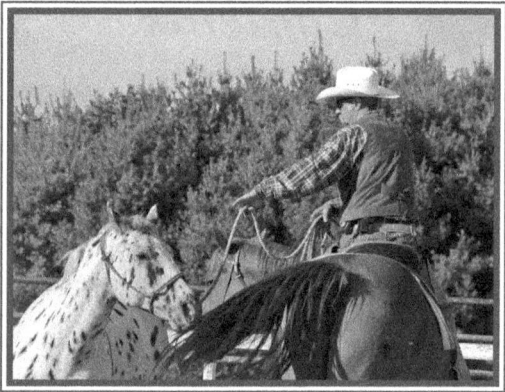

For more on Tom Moates, his books, and to contact him about his horsemanship clinics and lessons please visit www.TomMoates.com.

And be sure to check out Tom's Facebook page (www.facebook.com/ahorsesthought) where something is always happening!

Foreword One

The Christian Horseman's Companion is in no way intended to be a "how-to" book on horse training nor is it intended to be a theological book. It is intended to stimulate, encourage, and challenge us to think about the illustrations offered through the horse and human relationship as it pertains to and helps us grasp a deeper understanding and a greater appreciation for a relationship with God.

If Tom is anything he is truly sincere and serious about his relationship with both his God and Savior Jesus Christ as well as with his horses. He spends hours, days, weeks, and even years pondering ideas, situations, and life without losing sight of the innocence and simplicity of the truth. Tom is committed to truth, truth about the horse and more importantly the truth about God's Word, God's Character, and God's One and Only Son Jesus Christ!

He is a man I call a true friend with a sense of humor that keeps us entertained. I have spent many hours over the years answering questions and clarifying Biblical concepts and discussing illustrations offered by the horse and human relationship that might aid us in our understanding of the relationship between us and God. The danger in using the horse and human relationship to help us in our understanding of a relationship between God and man is the horse has no sin nature while humans continually struggle with rebellion, pride, and anger. Another danger is that humans aren't God! The God of Creation is All-Knowing, All-Powerful, and in the words of Tom, "All-Everything." I believe Tom has portrayed the possibilities of man's relationship with God using the illustrations of the horse and human without twisting the truth about either the horse or God.

I think *The Christian Horseman's Companion* can help us all grow in the grace and knowledge of our Lord and Savior Jesus Christ. My prayer is that you will be transformed by God through the renewing of your mind as you read this book.

In the Master's Hands,
Ronnie Moyer

Foreword Two

Tom labors over all he writes but this little book is his most meaningful labor yet. I hope you can get as much out of this book as Tom put into his labor to write it.

In it Tom has shared with us information to help us grow in our horsemanship and in our walk with Jesus Christ. This is a book I think you will read and re-read. You find scripture is like horsemanship as our experience and knowledge expands so too does our understanding of what is in the words and their meaning, so read, re-read, enjoy, learn, and grow.

Harry Whitney

Acknowledgements

A quick look at the Introduction and it should be clear that I have Harry Whitney, Ronnie Moyer, and my wife Carol Moates to thank for providing many of the key ingredients that made this book possible in the first place! I want to add a thanks to them for the time they spent going over the manuscript with me.

I want to thank Ava Dantis, Linda Davenport, and Catherine Millard for having a look at some of the chapters and providing some feedback as my working draft took shape.

I am very grateful to Carol Frazier Johnson for editing this book. Her careful reading of the manuscript and helpful comments were key to getting my earlier drafts into their refined form.

Thanks to Emily Kitching for providing layout insights and, in particular, for helping bring my vision for the cover to fruition.

A special thanks to all the photographers whose wonderful work contributes to this book: Teddy Carter, Danielle Gruber, Carol Moates, Mariah Petzoldt, Harry Whitney, and Olivia Wilkes.

I also want to send my appreciation to our local Thursday night Bible study group folks—while they still have not seen the book at this point as I prepare the final layout for the printer, that hasn't stopped them from being very supportive of the project over the past year and praying for the book and its author.

And, most importantly, I am eternally grateful to Our Heavenly Father for being "All-everything," for the amazing horses He created, for using horses to draw me to Him, and for allowing me the great gift of being able to explore His Word in so many wonderful ways!

Introduction

I came to Christ in no small way due to God's use of horses to draw me to Him. The trail I trod back then as I was just getting into horses seemed to have no clear path blazed ahead in any direction.

The twists and turns, this way and that, that I chose to take through the remote wilderness trail to salvation seem much more obvious in retrospect. Now those perceived forays into the wilds actually look more like rides along grand bridle paths with nice, well marked signs at all the intersections where I made hard turns or veered left or right at some of life's Ys.

Ah, perspective!

I say God used horses to draw me to Him, and that is accurate in a most immense way. But the underlying truth is that two horsemen made the real difference, and the horses were more of the means to get my mind to where it needed to be so that I could learn from these men, others, and the Bible. Again in retrospect, I see that God choreographed a seismic-life-shift for me that so perfectly fitted my needs—and yet was so far out of my life's regular orbit— that I am still left shuddering at the love He bestowed on this undeserving sinner.

First, I never experienced the compulsive disorder that is characteristic of the horse-obsessed person until my early 30s. It is a malady that typically has an early onset—teenage girls are particularly susceptible—and there is no known cure. When I came down with it, I got it really bad. My compulsive need to get better with horses prompted me to go way out of my comfort zone and do things that I otherwise never would have considered.

Second, honestly, I never would

have guessed—especially being the anti-Christian I was in my youth (I sadly relate to how Paul was Saul before becoming Paul)—that I could or would become a man of faith who studies the Word and openly confesses to be a follower of Jesus Christ. The fact that it happened is just one more way that God uses the least of us for His good work and proves that anyone can be saved.

So, let me name those two horsemen I mentioned above.

The first is my close friend and horsemanship mentor, Harry Whitney. The second is my close friend and Bible mentor, Ronnie Moyer.

It all began at about the time I was wrapping up my first horse book called *Discovering Natural Horsemanship*. I had quite literally completed that manuscript one day and was on a plane to meet Harry for the first time the next. We had discussed "picking up a soft feel" for an article I was writing for

Western Horseman magazine. I had interviewed many of the world's leading horsemanship clinicians and had pretty much wrapped it up when a friend suggested I call this fellow Harry. She passed along his phone number. When I spoke to Harry about the article I was blown away.

Harry was genuinely humble, and he sincerely worked to carefully select words that might help explain to me about horsemanship as he understood it, and he was truly trying hard to help me grasp what he was saying. It was not a typical interview for this equestrian journalist, and I was very much drawn to learn more from Harry.

Ultimately, after I had bombarded Harry with questions to a point probably past propriety (Harry is such a good sport!), Harry explained that horsemanship is difficult enough to work on when people are together with a horse right there to be seen. He offered that

I should come to his place in Arizona for a couple of weeks of clinics so that we could better discuss some aspects of horsemanship in person and with some horses to help. To make a long story short, with my wife Carol urging me on, I jumped completely out of my regular orbit and comfort zone, booked a ticket, and went.

I nearly didn't make it. The trip from Virginia out to Arizona ended up taking two days rather than one due to a series of confounding setbacks. I came so close to packing it in and just going back home that it's a wonder I didn't. How different my life would be today if that had happened! There are 10 horse books (well, 11 if you count this one) and literally hundreds of articles I've written that would not exist in the form that they do. The horsemanship I have learned from Harry that I now teach would not be with me to underpin my livelihood or truly help me to help horses and people

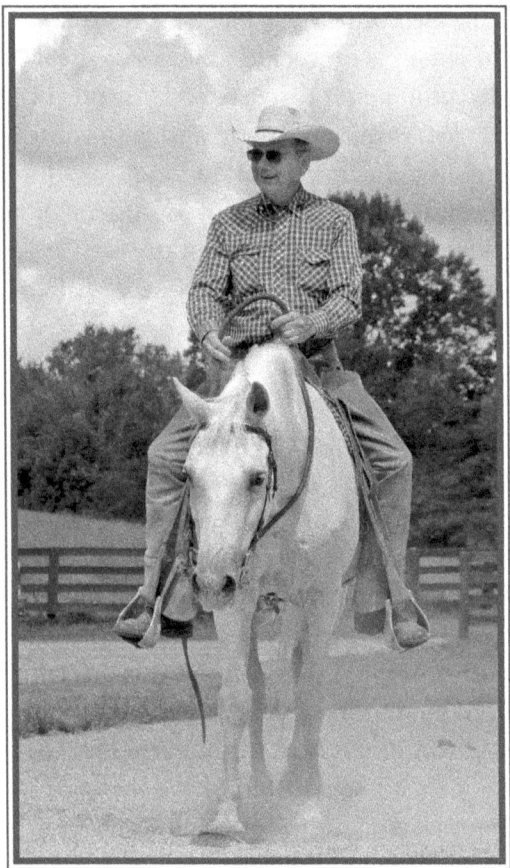

Harry Whitney.

to the depth that I now can. But most importantly, God was at work.

I went out there a non-believer, and I returned as one—at least I think I did. My movement towards becoming a believer unfolded over some years yet to come, and I really have no clear idea of just when it took place. There certainly was no flash to it. Rather, the transition seemed to gain momentum over time until I no longer could deny Christ. But my serious Christian-walk beginnings are firmly linked to that trip because without it, I would not have been on the path that has led me here, and it represents a very clear turn from one general direction to another. It was a threshold I crossed where everything began to change—my thinking changed—however slowly.

I had discovered from meeting Harry face-to-face that my suspicions about him had been correct. He was genuine, and genuinely in the horsemanship deal to help the horses and their humans rather than to use the horses as a way to campaign for himself. I doubt I've met a man with more empathy for horses than Harry. And getting to know him better led me to understand a major factor that was different about him from so many other horsemen that I had met, and that was his strong Christian faith—his relationship with God.

I soon realized that Harry's faith in Jesus Christ was one of the main factors behind who he was, how he acted, and how he was getting such amazing results with horses. It was all intertwined, and I wanted to know more about it.

Harry had told me about the Bible/horsemanship clinics he taught in tandem with a fella named Ronnie Moyer. I really wanted to go to one, but they were being held in California at that time (and they still are), and a few had been hosted in Arizona and Colorado. I was back home in Virginia without the

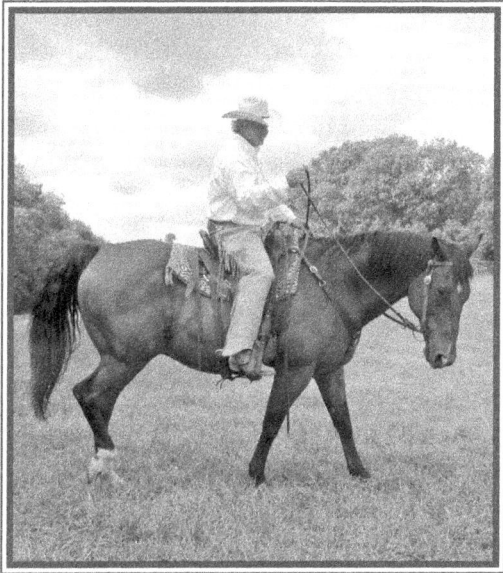

Ronnie Moyer.

means to go traveling out west again at that point. Also, Carol's health was deteriorating and she was facing a liver transplant. Yet it was Carol who did the prompting to set up getting Harry and Ronnie to come to Virginia and teach a Bible/horsemanship clinic here.

It was her idea to host them here so that I would be able to experience one of those clinics. Incredibly, (I still marvel at God's hand in this) even as Carol sat right near the top of the transplant list, it all came together, and that clinic was held within a year of my inaugural trip to Arizona to meet Harry. That was a dozen years ago. Carol ended up having not one but two back-to-back liver transplants, and my faith in God made huge strides as I witnessed prayers answered time after time during her long recovery. She got back on her feet, has done extremely well, and remains very healthy to this day. And the Virginia Bible/horsemanship clinic has been running annually ever since. Some years back it grew from one week to two, and each year in late August we meet here in Floyd, Virginia, to study the Word, improve our horsemanship, fellowship, and fundraise for Moyer Ministries.

I met Ronnie at that first Virginia

clinic. Meeting Ronnie was another
one of those moments where my life
gained something new and substantial.
Ronnie was a bullfighter—that is, he was
working in rodeos during bull ridings to
help distract the bulls after the bull riders
"dismounted" (one way or another). He
owned a ranch in Colorado and ran
Moyer Ministries with his wife Becky.
Again, here was a man whom I soon had
much respect for who truly lived his life
in a way that I was not accustomed to
seeing—a man who really believed in
the Bible as truth and put that Word into
the reality of his choices. I was stunned,
really, since I couldn't remember in my
life being provided such examples before.

Mostly, I am grateful that—as with
learning horsemanship from the early
stages on with a remarkable horseman
such as Harry—my Christian walk was
guided by a cowboy chaplain such as
Ronnie Moyer.

I remember distinctly attending

church as a young person, and even an adult, and being very uncomfortable asking questions. I always got the impression that asking questions was viewed as a slight to the teachers in church—that somehow it represented insubordination or lack of faith or some negative thing. That was never the case with Ronnie (poor Ronnie, taking the brunt of my inquisitive mind when it came to the Bible).

I could ask all the important questions I had without some weird vibe. And what impressed me was not that he answered them, but that when he answered, he drew the answers from scripture. Sometimes with questions during Bible clinics he even had to go do some research to discover what scripture said about a question before he answered. And if Ronnie was interjecting his own opinion into an answer, he would always let us know that it was his thinking on a subject and not something he had found in scripture.

Observing this approach to getting questions answered by searching God's answers to them in scripture has pointed me in the right direction for my own growth. And pretty early on after I began attending Bible/horsemanship clinics, I became way more confident... not in my own knowledge and wisdom, but certainly in where I can go to find God's truth and input on subjects that is provided for us humans, the Bible.

Suffice it to say that God used horses to draw me to these two men, and they have been the pivotal influence in my opening the Bible and doing a better job of living by that Living Word—and especially in my getting the big one: coming to faith in Jesus Christ as the Son of God who was sacrificed for the sins of the world for all time, was resurrected, and lives.

As I mentioned before, there has never been some single big momentous event for me where suddenly everything was different—bang! No, for me it has been many shifts over time, and I still have my struggles. But my relationship with Christ is out of the first saddling phase. The cinches are tight, and I do seem to have quit all that bucking, at least! The reins also seem to have some meaning to me now, and I'm finding that His thoughts are more readily directing my thoughts as time goes on.

The Christian Horseman's Companion exists that I might share with you some of what has been profoundly helpful to me as I've gained some scriptural understandings, particularly when my work with horses has provided excellent insights. I hope that you, too, will find these musings valuable, and that perhaps my sharing some of how God has used horses in my life might be a benefit and a blessing to you, too.

Chapter One

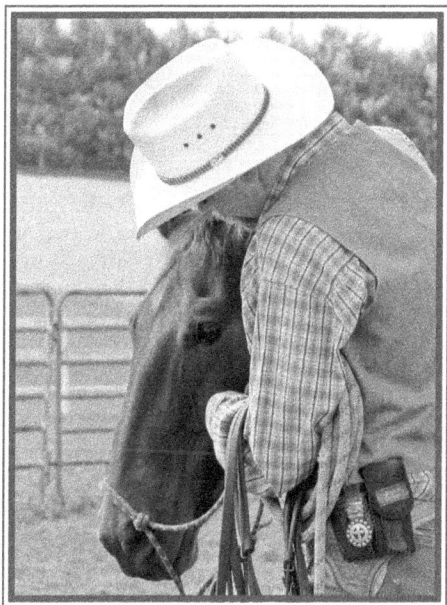

"You will keep him in perfect peace whose mind is stayed on You because he trusts You." Isaiah 26:3

The mind.

The round pen panels rattled violently as the hefty horse thrust his chest against the gate. The handsome, sorrel equine had been trotting back and forth along that part of the round pen fence since being turned loose in the pen a few minutes earlier. Back and forth he went repeatedly, until he threw his head up as high as it would go and again pushed hard into the gate with his chest—clang, clang!

God has provided us many great benefits in the horse. Climbing atop a horse provided humans the first chance to travel overland faster than our own flat feet could carry us. What a revolution and advantage it was to the human world, and a mind-altering change of reality to boot, when people, stuff, and information began to travel at speeds well beyond that of what people could accomplish afoot. But as one who has had horses play an instrumental role in his salvation, I'm here to share with you that by using the horse, God has provided man some of the very best opportunities to gain scriptural insights that exist on our blue planet. Consider the scene I began describing above.

The reason horses sometimes act the way this horse did was clear to me. This insight came to me via my friend and horsemanship clinician Harry Whitney. Harry had explained to me and to others at his clinics which I had attended over the years that the underlying reason for horses' behaviors (and why things go poorly or well between them and humans) lies in where their minds are focused.

In fact, pretty much everything short of physical issues in a horse boils down to this very point. As Harry is fond of saying, "When a horse's mind and his body are not in the same place at the same time, there's trouble in the household!" Standing there in the round

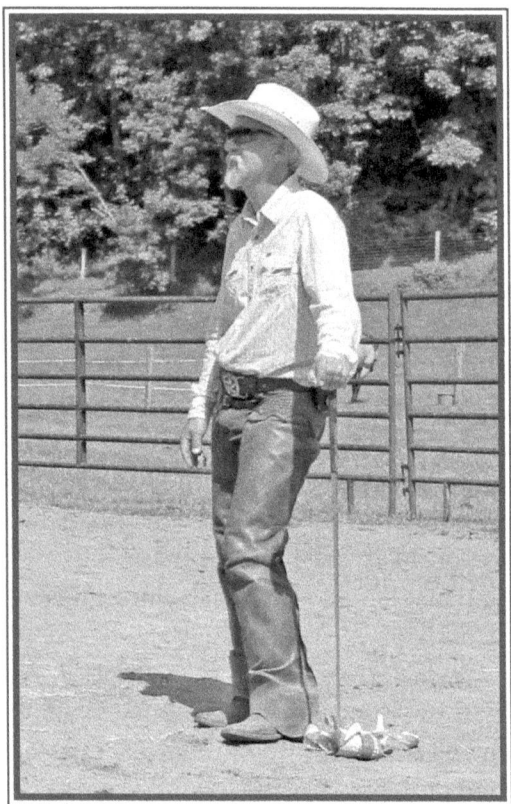

I stand in a round pen with a flag while working a horse during the Floyd, Virginia Bible/horsemanship clinic in 2014.

corral with this horse, it was easy to see that there was trouble in his household.

I stood with a training flag in the center of the round pen, watching the gelding struggle with his predicament. A crowd stood around one half of the round pen in the drizzle watching the horse and me. I had just given a talk to these trail riding enthusiasts about horsemanship, and now I was giving a demonstration of the kind of horsemanship I practice and teach. The horse belonged to one of the folks there.

The gelding chose to hover around the gate and push against it because, in part, he knew that it was the way out of that pen. Even more so, he was intent on that spot because the gate happened to be the closest point between him and his equine buddy who was penned, in sight, about 50 feet away in an arena.

"Notice how distraught he is?" I asked the crowd. "Am I of any importance to him? Does he even see me?"

Clang! The gelding pushed his chest against the gate again.

"Well, I can guarantee you he knows I'm in this pen with him," I answered one of my own questions. "Horses don't miss much in their environments. But he is ignoring me. I'm of no importance to him. In a moment I'm going to suggest in a fairly big way that he take more notice of me. The problem here is that his mind is with his buddy over there. I visualize that his brain has popped out of his head, bounced over the fence, and is literally over there by his friend. He is trying hard to get his body over there to where his brain is, but the panels are in the way."

In a flash I raised the flag over my head and came down hard against the ground in a quick kerwhackow!

The horse took off at a high rate of speed and began to run the whole circumference of the round pen. Around

and around me he ran until he decided
to go back to doing what he was doing
before...going back-and-forth worriedly
along the gate and panels closest to his
buddy.

My position in the middle of the pen
had put me behind the horse when his
concentration was focused outside of the
pen onto the horse in the arena. Thus, my
kerwhackow! had disrupted his intense
focus, and he had brought his thought
back into the pen to deal with the
disruption behind him. That moment
was such a colossal interruption of his
hard focus that he had responded in a
big way. That big reaction represented a
change in his mind. At that moment, the
flagging meant that he had to take much
greater notice of me behind him inside
the pen—and although it was done with
considerable duress and running on his
part, it was, at least, a change of thought.
It was the beginning of the work I
would do to establish and improve our

relationship, which in turn I would use to get him to feel better inside of himself.

I observed him making decisions on his own for a few minutes. It may not have been observable to the crowd, but I was presenting an idea to the horse that he should come over to me and find that I was offering a sweet spot between us for him to focus on and a chance for him to find rest and peace. But, the gelding didn't know much about this yet. His instincts and experiences ruled his behavior and emotions. He just kept running along his favorite section of the fence, thinking across the way to his buddy, pining to get there.

Back-and-forth, back-and-forth. Clang!

Kerwhackow! I flagged another time.

Off he went running the whole way around the round pen again at a high rate of speed. His head was jacked way up and his nose was tipped outwards as he more-or-less kept concentrating outside of the pen. But again, this speedy tearing all the way around the pen represented a change of thought. He was taking more notice of me which meant he had to be letting go of the strangle-hold on the thought of getting out of the pen and over to his equine buddy, even if he was having a fit about it.

The scenario repeated again, but this time rather than gravitating back to his favorite part of the fence, he kept on running all the way around the pen. I pointed this out to the crowd—that it was a change, but that he remained greatly unsettled.

How often do we find ourselves running a race in life, trying to get our bodies to where are minds are? This horse easily represents a person who wants to get to the store, to an appointment, to work, to finish a project, to pick up the kids...rush, rush, rush, always thinking about where we need to be next rather than where we are. Even if it's all good stuff that we're wanting to get to—to a game, to Bible study, to volunteer somewhere—trying to be there already when we're not there yet, especially if we are late, can be stressful and we can feel like we're trapped behind some panels. Chasing dollars, chasing entertainment, chasing health, chasing whatever...the behavior and mental state of the horse in the round pen that day provided a pretty good visible representation of what goes on inside of us humans sometimes.

In this modern age, we even have electronic devices that potentially add to this troubled state of mind like cell phones that we carry with us everywhere to make sure that we're always focused on all these other places, people, and thoughts that aren't where we are at the moment. We pay monthly fees to be provided with distractions that can keep our minds and bodies widely separated. People can get so frantic that they really don't think about the moment regardless of where they are, and some may even develop a frantic pace in life to straight-up avoid looking closely at their lives.

Part of the bother in this situation, as we see in both the frantic horse and frantic people, is that the creature is attempting to solve his own troubles. How does a horse solve the problem of being contained in a corral he can't get out of to go be with his herd mate? He can't do it alone—he needs to be set free. Likewise, how do we solve the troubling issues in our lives ourselves? If it were within our power to do so, wouldn't people just let themselves out of their predicaments, and we'd all be supremely happy every day? Of course we would. But the truth is that we can't do it ourselves—we, too, need to be set free by someone else.

To get to the real root of this dilemma, it is essential to understand that the answer to the horse's predicament that day in the round pen was not simply to set him free from the confines of the round pen so he could go over to be with his buddy. That's not really freedom from what ails the poor creature since if we separated the two again, he'd just return to his troubled racing and banging. In fact, it might even get worse since it would be proving to the horse that all that tension and violent activity got him set loose. There is no personal growth in that for the horse—letting him loose from the pen would be a mechanical, temporary fix providing us with a momentarily happy horse who would do the very same thing again.

If you wanted to take that horse on a trail ride away from other horses and have him be okay and safe, what options then do you have? Taking the buddy with you everywhere you ever go? Is that really a solution? No, it's not. In the same way buying new things, overeating, gambling, and on-and-on never really solve a person's troubles either, but rather momentarily fill some emotional hole, and then it's right back to the troubles again.

From my position in the center of the pen, I picked a spot about 110 degrees to the left of the gate (just outside of the range of his favorite zone), and, as he flew past this spot running full circles around me, I flagged once, just slightly.

This caused the horse to bolt past me even faster.

"I'm not doing this to ask him to run harder," I explained to the folks watching, because it might have seemed so.

The gelding was running along the fence counter clockwise, and, as he came to that same spot along the panels again, I flagged once again from my position in the center of the pen. Again, he ripped forward even harder.

"I'm flagging at one particular spot as he goes around me to get him to think about it," I continued. "Now watch what happens."

A third time looked much like the first two as he came by that point—I flagged, and he squirted past. But the fourth time, just as he approached the point where I was going to flag, yet before I did, he hit the brakes, spun a 180, and went back the other direction. He ran the whole way around the pen in the other direction and as he approached my chosen flag-spot, again he threw on the brakes, turned in, and stopped, facing me.

He stood there looking at me— really looking at me—for the first time since the session had begun. The horse was thinking "here" for the first time. He had gone from having his brain completely outside the pen over on his buddy, to racing around inside the pen just wanting to escape, to finally finding a spot where he could settle a moment, really take in his immediate surroundings, and think. It also was the first time he had felt like he could stop moving his feet.

His mind, for the first time since we began, was stayed on me.

I had been offering this spot between us the whole time—even from before I flagged the first time. That is not something people can see. I explained that I was offering in my mind and with my energy for him to come, be with me, focus his mind with me in the center of the pen, quit all that running and busy-ness, relax, and have peace. But he wasn't able to hear the offer because he was mentally too far gone and bent on trying to figure things out himself. And without his being with-me, there was no way I could help him feel better, let alone direct him so that we might do some tasks together.

The mind.

His mind was now stayed on me, at least for a moment, and that allowed the gelding to stop thinking about his friend in the other pen. With his brain back in his head and his thoughts finally focused right there with his body in the pen, he could settle a bit and begin to think about what was going on between us.

What a difference.

I had seen Harry do this kind of work with a loose horse in a corral a bunch of times over the years. By the time I was giving this demonstration, I, too, had done this with many horses over many years, so I was pretty confident to predict to the audience the outcome of what was about to take place each step of the way. In the realm of horsemanship, this kind of intervention often can help provide the great advantage of helping a horse to get "with you," as Harry says. But, in the realm of scriptural understanding, it was Ronnie Moyer working with Harry through Bible/horsemanship clinics that got me thinking about this in another way. They used examples of man's relationship to horses in the round pen like this to provide what I believe is one of the best and most helpful examples of God's relationship to man that exists. At least, it has proven to be so for this horse-obsessed horseman.

Before proceeding, I want to caution that we must not go overboard and misinterpret what I'm about to say. This is merely an awesome illustration, but one where man plays the role of God in relationship to the horse, who plays the part of the human in the round pen, and the reality is certainly that man is not God, and horses do not have a sin nature as do people. So, let's be sure to keep this real, soak in the lesson, and apply it in the proper perspective.

* * *

That one quiet moment with the gelding in the round pen wasn't the end of the theatrics. I moved off to one side to see if the horse could draw closer to me, but he had to leave me and go out and run the fence some more. I just kept reminding him by making a little noise and occasionally using the flag slightly that I was right there in the center of the pen. I offered that he could stop the ceaseless battle of trying to figure out this predicament on his own at any time. I was working to put him in a situation where he understood it was within his power to chose to quit the running around wishing to be somewhere else. That he could come in close to me—and that stopping and being with me would be a restful and safe haven that would feel better to him than anything else he had experienced so far in that pen.

With some flagging interventions, increasingly the horse turned and came towards me several more times until he would stand close to me, and I could reach out and stroke his face. Before long, I could walk off and he would

My mare Mirage approached me after some work with the flag at liberty in the round pen, and I offer a sweet spot as she stands calmly close to me.

follow me willingly. He was becoming so relaxed that I could stop, turn to him, and pet his face a stroke or two and then walk on with the horse in tow. His head was down and he was breathing less hard, recuperating from all of the running and worrying he had done.

"You will keep him in perfect peace whose mind is stayed on You because he trusts You." Isaiah 26:3

There is so much in this example to relate to how God and man interact, and many verses of scripture that can be applied to add insights to some of the examples. As one who knows that Jesus Christ is the Son of God who was sacrificed for the sins of the world on the cross and was resurrected, I likewise know the Holy Bible is the living Word of God. So it is to the Bible I look when I want to know what God has to say about things. Over the years as I studied horsemanship, I also was studying the Bible, and scriptures grabbed me when they fit with the horse work. I came to write this book by saving these connections in notebooks because I wanted to remember them and to share them with others. Isaiah 26:3 is a big one, and seems like a great place to start. I also had the benefit of Ronnie's teaching where he pointed out some of the scriptures that apply to horsemanship, as well. This is why I will point to scripture and share passages as they relate to the horse work throughout this book.

What a change in the horse in the round pen that day. To go from being in a near panic and pushing on the gate with his chest, to running like a maniac, to focusing on me and relaxing a great deal, to following me. This process makes sense to me today. I am not one whose acceptance of Christ as my Lord and Savior came in a single flash—a moment where I was suddenly changed that I can point to and say, "It happened right then!" Mine was much more gradual. It grew stronger as the Lord flagged me over and over and over, drawing me to Him. It was like God was in the middle of the round pen of my life, and I was the horse running like crazy with my thoughts anywhere except on Him, let alone in the pen. It even is accurate to say that I experienced a time where I knew Jesus was the Lord, I accepted that as fact, but I actively avoided a relationship with Him, not yet ready to turn from embracing my sinful ways even though I knew the Truth.

"For no one can come to me unless the Father who sent me draws them to me...."
John 6:44

When I became acquainted with John 6:44, round pen examples like the one above crystallized in my mind (on some level, at least) what it may be like for God to desire to draw us into a relationship with Him. I knew the gelding would take stronger notice of me when I flagged him, he would begin to acknowledge me, and he would eventually warm up to me because his mind would focus with me there in the pen. I wasn't sure how long it would take...but I was confident in the ultimate outcome and the basic course the conversation would take. I allowed the horse the freedom to search within that round pen so when he decided to try coming to me, he knew that, within the options open to him, the decision had been his and he needn't be resentful or feel trapped about it. This example really helped me to understand how God can at once be in control and draw us to Him, and yet not violate our free will to make choices.

In looking over my life I can see where the Lord has flagged me here and there. He never forced me to follow Him, but he patiently offered that instead of running around in the world, worrying about and indulging in all its evils and perils, that I could turn and face Him—that I draw towards Him with my mind and find perfect peace there.

Isaiah 26:3 also adds trust to the equation. The gelding obviously did

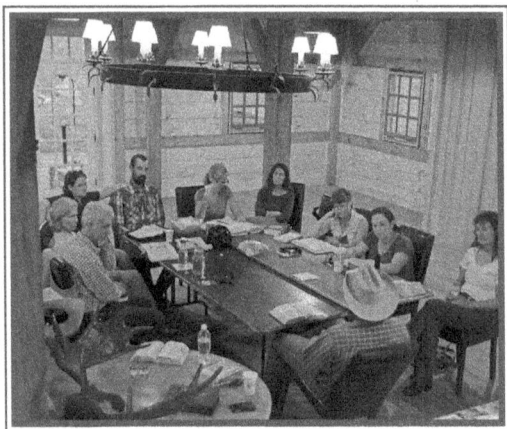

Bible study in the barn at the 2014 Virginia Bible/
horsemanship clinic.

not trust me at first. In fact, he pretty
much ran the range of other options in
the pen to do whatever he could to get
out of there and away from me. That
dubious outlook towards me represents
the opposite of trust. But, with some
well-timed flagging and a persistent offer
of a sweet spot, the gelding began to see
things differently.

The whole time, he wanted to feel better. He was going about looking for relief in the way his experience and hard wiring told him he should. This reminds me of the world's lies that tell us that running after things—more money, other people, a new car, prestige, power—is the answer to our worries and problems. But God says, trust Him, stay your mind on Him, and He will keep you in perfect peace. When the horse was able to keep his mind stayed on me, only then were his thoughts not on his buddy or on how to escape the round pen, and that is when he was able to settle and find some peace.

As I said earlier, so many scriptures can be applied to this round pen example. At this point, I want to share Proverbs 1:7:

"Fear of the Lord is the foundation of true knowledge...."

Did the gelding fear me at first? Certainly, he did. That is why he reacted by trying to flee and escape my presence. But, after that initial fear, the horse gained the true knowledge that he need not run to escape me nor the pen. The truth was that he could feel at peace right there. And that opportunity had existed the whole time from the very beginning of the session. I never said to that horse, "Hey you, horse, get out there and run around those panels!" No, from the moment I set foot in the pen I already was offering that he should come to the middle and be relaxed and calm with me even though he was blinded to it at the time. Isn't that what God offers us right now and always? That at any moment we can turn to Him. Jesus says in Matthew 11:28:

"Come to Me, all of you who are weary and carry heavy burdens, and I will give you rest."

That doesn't say "Stop by on Tuesdays between 12:00 and 2:00 p.m., and I'll help you out." It just says, "Come to Me all who are weary and carry heavy burdens...." That's anyone at anytime, no strings attached. That can be hard for us to believe; however, it is true.

The gelding did not believe it at first, to be sure. But when he underwent the fearful experience of having to face the facts that I was in the pen, getting big-ish, going to interact with him, and actually in control of his circumstances, he became a believer. With freedom to make choices within the round pen still intact, the gelding decided that coming to me was an option he should try. As he did, he discovered that it was a good one where he'd find rest. And what a change in his world for the better to know that he could trust me to be there for him, and that he could let go of his worries and be at peace with me there.

I often see round-penning a horse

done in another way that I do not agree with. There are those who like to get into a round pen with a horse and chase the horse around the pen.

Notice in the example with the gelding that I simply stood in the center of the pen and offered that the horse draw his mind and body to me so that he could discover that to be with me provided him a good feeling and rest. I never asked the horse to run or move around the pen at that point, other than to come and stand quietly by me; all that running around was his idea and choice.

This other round-penning method I want to mention, however, makes the horse so miserable by running him hard around the pen that when the person stops and backs off, it sucks the horse into that vacuum. In my mind, this method of driving the horse around (even though it may bring a horse to a person much sooner than the way I worked it above) takes away the horse's options and freedom of choice. That fact has consequences regarding how the horse thinks and feels about the person and the situation.

A horse like the one in the pen with me that day already feels lousy and on high alert just by being trapped in a scary situation. If a person adds to that by bringing a horse's flee instinct way up to the point that he has to run because he is fleeing from the person, and then the human suddenly stops pushing the horse and draws him in that way, well...why does the horse come to the person? The horse approaches the person not because he wants to be with the one who has been chasing him, but only because in a pinch it seems better than being chased. The horse, no doubt, feels terrible to be near the person in this situation, but he knows it feels worse being made to run along the panels. It puts a horse between a rock and a hard spot. I don't want to be my horse's hard spot; I want to be his sweet spot where he experiences comfort, security, and rest.

God is faithful, and He "means what He says and says what He means," as Ronnie is fond of saying.

When I entered the round pen with this horse, I knew where our relationship would end up—that he would acknowledge me, begin to search for me, and start to feel better about things along the way because of the relationship that I instigated. I did not know how long it would take or exactly what I might do to get there because the horse had the freedom to explore his options within the round pen. But I knew I had the tools to get the horse to begin to think, to consider a relationship with me, and to begin to feel better about things. And I knew I was willing to follow through faithfully to get a change for the better in this horse.

I had an Aha! moment when Ronnie

and Harry began to share that one can think of God as being in the center of our round pen—our world—looking at us lovingly as we work up a sweat, back-and-forth we go, smashing into the fence panels of our lives, but that God loves us enough to set things up so that we can change. And He's willing to see it through with great patience, even though because of our actions, we deserve none of it. God flags us. He says, "Hey, fella, let that thought go, come stand by Me, get rest, and know peace."

As a believer, I look to God's Word for understanding and clarity in life. It was Ronnie who pointed out to me John 6:44, and it was a round pen example like the one above that really made it stick in my mind. Look at it again:

> *"For no one can come to me unless the Father who sent me draws them to me...."*
> *John 6:44*

What better way to think about how God may draw us to Him than to consider how we may draw a horse to us in a small corral where we are clearly right there to be seen? Especially for one who is well acquainted with horses, this example shows how profound and quick a change for the better can occur when we let go of chasing what we think we need and begin to see what God has in mind for us..."perfect peace." As with the gelding, this shift occurs in the mind and has everything to do with our focus.

The mind!

Chapter Two

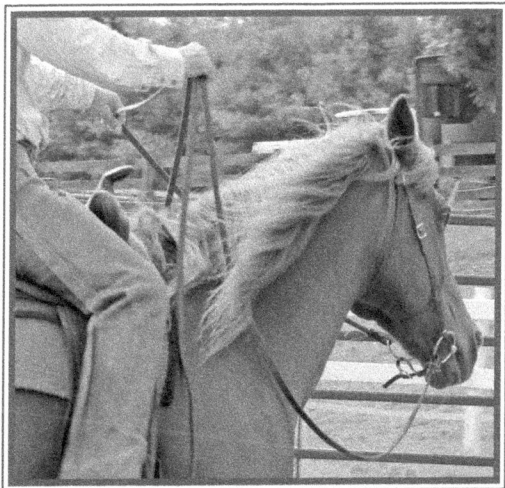

"Don't copy the behavior and customs of this world, but let God transform you into a new person by changing the way you think." Romans 12:2

I love the first sentence of Romans 12:2. This is a verse I have memorized and can recite—although I am the first to admit that I struggle with getting scripture to stick verbatim in my mind. A quick glance at this verse is all it takes to see that it continues to build on what we started in the previous chapter.

Romans 12:2 tells us that we must not "copy the behaviors and customs of this world." In the realm of horses, I see this in the actions of the gelding in the round pen from my earlier example.

God says, do not go out there and participate in and chase after all those things that the world holds in high esteem. Or, for the horse, do not go and long to be over in the other pen, back at the barn, or generally fixate on other worries.

The second part of the first sentence of this verse is one that I find crucial to understand. It is helpful in comprehending the very essence of how

our relationship with God works. Look
carefully at it:

*"...let God transform you into a new person
by changing the way you think."*

It says that God transforms us, so it
is God who does the transforming and
not we who do it, and it thereby confirms
that a transformation in us is possible.
It says to "let" God transform us, so
God is offering this transformation all
the time, just as I was offering from the
very beginning of the round pen session
for the gelding to come to me and find
rest and peace. God's offer is always
there, but we need to recognize it, to
turn to Him, and to accept His offer of
transformation.

It seems simple, and when I look at
the transformation in the horse, I know
that in a way it is. But also, as I saw in
the gelding, it is very hard to let go of
what we think we know...of what the

world is telling us to do.

And now for one of those huge Biblical realizations that flagged me upside the head when I read it, "...by changing the way you think."

How does God transform worldly people into new, more Christ-like people? By changing how we think.

Reflect on the horse in the round pen. What changed in that scenario? Not the round pen. Not the buddy horse or the arena he was in. Not where I was standing. Not the weather. Not the number or placement of people watching. Not anything, really, accept some well-timed flag whacks and how that horse was thinking. The real shift occurred in his mind. That new thinking, in turn, changed how he felt, and that then changed his actions for the better for all to see.

What does it take for a person to change course and see that a better life

exists for him or her? A simple example
I often see is reflected in when I get calls
from new clients to come and help them
with their horses. A normal scenario
is that a person calls for assistance who
has had a wreck or is otherwise having
difficulties with a horse. Horse people
tend to become ready to change the way
they are doing things with a horse when
they feel in danger, or at the very least,
are unable to do what they want to with
a horse. Horse people are not unique
in this. We all are guilty of not making
positive changes until we get in trouble
or feel flagged. The Bible states this fact
with forthright clarity:

*"None is righteous, no, not one;
no one understands; no one seeks for
God. All have turned aside; together
they have become worthless;
no one does good, not even one."*
Romans 3:10-12

There you have it—no one seeks God; no one does good, not even one. That includes every one of us humans. Which brings us full circle to a previous point we looked into, that it is God who draws us to Him to bring about change in our lives, like I drew the gelding to me in the round pen to bring about change in how he was thinking, feeling, and acting. We don't seek God; it is He who seeks a relationship with us.

The kind of horse work we have been looking at proves that it is possible for a horse to relax and find peace in a situation where it never dawned on him that he could. This possibility exists even if he doesn't know it. Even before the offer is realized, or even if it never is realized, it remains a real offer.

In our example, before the horse knew me, he did not know letting go of his strong thoughts, being with a person, and relaxing was an option. I was the one who knew what was possible for him

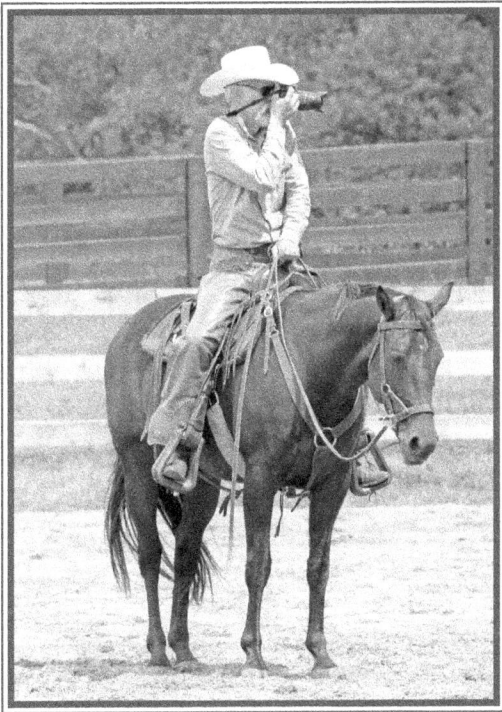

It is possible for a horse, like Mirage, to relax and find peace in a situation where it never would have dawned on her that she could before some capable human intervention—like standing still in a busy arena while I take pictures of the action from the saddle.

and that he could leave those distractions and worries behind and be transformed to a much more relaxed horse. Even after the gelding met me, and my flag a time or two, he still wasn't ready to hear what I was offering. But I was patient and kept reminding him, "Hey horse, it'll sure be better for you if you let that go and come over to be with me and find rest." Ultimately, it was his relationship with me that changed his situation for the better—but our pairing up was not what he would have chosen without my intervention on his behalf.

So, what was in that deal with the gelding for me? Was standing in the rain working a horse in the round pen a better deal for me in some ways than being at home in a warm, dry house writing, canning tomatoes, or whatever? Was I about to undergo a big personal transformation brought on by working this horse? No. But, I love horses, and I absolutely enjoy seeing one make a change for the better. It gives me profound joy. Zephaniah 3:17 (yes, a rarely quoted book of the Bible, to be sure—but I love finding gold nuggets along the scriptural trail less traveled) gives insight into this:

"For the Lord your God is living among you. He is a mighty Savior. He will take delight in you with gladness. With His love, He will calm all your fears."

God is in the middle of our round pen...right there, close all the time; He is "living among you." You delight Him. He, because He loves you, will calm all your fears with His love. Our Heavenly Father "is a mighty Savior" who saves us from our sinful selves.

This passage lines up so well with my round pen example that it is self-explanatory—but I like how it injects God's love into the mix. "With His love," He calms us. Thus, we know that He loves us, and that is why He is in the round pen with us helping us to find peace. My love for helping horses made standing in the rain helping one, and sharing some helpful horsemanship with other folks, a better deal for me than my personal comforts.

This makes me turn to one of the more quoted verses from the Bible, one that deeply moved me the first time I read it and that I still can not read without feeling the effect of its gravity pulling on me:

"Love is patient and kind. Love is not jealous or boastful or proud or rude. It does not demand its own way. It is not irritable, and it keeps no record of being wronged. It does not rejoice about injustice but rejoices whenever the truth wins out. Love never gives up, never loses faith, is always hopeful, and endures through every circumstance." 1 Corinthians 13:4-7

If it is our love for the horse that has us in the round pen helping him to let go of his anxieties and to find peace with us, this verse explains what that really looks like. We will be patient...offering that the horse find us and leave his worries behind, but not demanding that to happen. If it takes awhile, we must not become irritable, and certainly must not count it against the horse if by his being a horse he does things in the course of our work with him that seem like wrongs made against us. (It is not personal for the horse.) We endure through the circumstances with faith that the horse will get to a better spot.

There are many reasons a person might benefit from having a relaxed and willing horse. That horse becomes more useful, more valuable monetarily, and safer. However, it takes spending a lot of time and energy to get better with horses to be able to bring about such changes if we are looking for a deeper horsemanship than mere mechanical methods produce. To be honest, getting really through to the horse's mind and making a truly peaceful, willing partner of a horse is difficult enough that the worldly benefits are hardly incentive enough to stick it out if you aren't doing it first for the love and compassion of the horse.

Okay, so now that I've talked about love, we need to circle back and put this in the proper perspective. God's love calms our fear, but He works this by changing the way we think. It is very easy, especially in the culture of our western world today, to look for God to transforms us through an emotional experience—by the way we feel. But Romans 12:2 clearly explains that God transforms us by changing the way we think. Our transformation, like that of the horse in the round pen, occurs in the mind. That isn't to say there can be no emotional by-product to the transformation, but the scripture rightly places the pivot point of achieving perfect peace on a change of thought rather than some emotional experience.

Here's another often-quoted scripture that can help guide our understanding of this:

> *"Trust in the Lord with all your heart and do not lean on your own understanding. In all your ways acknowledge Him, and He will make your paths straight."*
> *Proverbs 3:5-6*

Our own understanding is like that of the horse in the round pen at first—it is of the world and driven by desires that result from our being in the flesh. The truly seismic shift comes from discovering that we can refocus our minds away from that worrisome course, acknowledge God in our own round pen, and He will "make our paths straight." In other words, God can line us out to a truly good and profitable path—His desire for us all—that we never could accomplish on our own because our own understanding is so corrupted.

Let's let God wrap up this chapter and have His Word speak to us and soak into our minds with another verse that seems to fit here perfectly:

"I am leaving you with a gift—peace of mind and heart. And the peace I give is a gift the world cannot give. So don't be troubled or afraid." John 14:27

Chapter Three

"*So prepare your minds for action and exercise self-control.*" *1 Peter 1:13*

The mind.

Yes, again we circle back to thoughts and thinking, but it is because scripture brings us back to the importance of the mind over and over again. In this chapter's verse, Peter calls us to action.

Horses, of course, are not people, so not all of the human experiences and insights covered in scripture will fit sensibly into equine examples. This is one of those. A horse can't be told to go prepare his mind. Well, I suppose you could tell your horse that, and he might even look at you for a moment with those big, intelligent eyes before he went back to cluelessly munching his hay or whatever he was doing before you spoke.

This is one of those deals where humans' command of language allows for a special relationship with God that is beyond the capacity of animals to enjoy. God's Word has bearing on us because He engages us through language. But there remains a great horse lesson in this verse nonetheless.

When I came across this verse, I immediately thought of how humans approach horses. This first thing that sprang to my mind was how angry some people get at horses, and how counter-productive that is.

I see people get angry at horses when horses do not do what they are "supposed" to do. I think this anger is often rooted in the misbelief that the horse is doing something against the person on purpose. This couldn't be farther from the truth, but it is our minds that perpetuate this lie. It is essential to alter that way of thinking if we are to understand correctly and help our equine friends feel better about our relationship with them and for them to become willing partners. If we are going to work in the most productive way possible with our horses, we must "prepare our minds for action and exercise self-control."

It boils down to two facts: one, that horses do not possess a sin nature. (That is a purely human characteristic.) And two, that we humans project onto the horse human traits. (This is called anthropomorphizing.)

Horses do not have a sin nature as man does. Rather, horses operate under motivations like the over-riding, hard-wired instinct to protect themselves at all costs or to seek comfort. Instincts like self-preservation can produce behavior that people wrongly interpret as being slights made against them personally.

Take an example as simple as a person trying to get a horse to circle around him. The horse might throw a shoulder into the person. The person reads that as the horse being a bully, intentionally trying to push or even hurt him. The reality could be that there is something out in the environment that the human may not even sense, like a chickadee in the bushes that just might be a horse-eating chickadee. (They are rare but you never know, so better to be prepared.) In that mindset, the horse may feel the need to push the person out of his mental and physical space so that he can concentrate on the potential danger and be prepared to flee to save himself if he needs to.

Or perhaps the horse mentally is just trying to escape being engaged by the person and is displacing his thoughts out away from the person. In this case, the horse may quite literally be trying to push a person out of his mental space with his shoulder as he looks strongly away, wishing to be somewhere else. This is much like the mindset of the horse in the round pen in the example from the first chapter who was wanting to be with his buddy and ignoring me at first.

Even if the horse really is focused on the person and pushes him just to see if he can, which can be the behavior between horses jockeying for position in the herd, that still is just an innocent horse being a horse—it is not a horse who got up that morning and said to himself, "That stupid Tom Moates! He fed me late last night so I'll show him. I'll step on his foot and then knock him down for that, the sorry bugger!"

People do that kind of thing, not horses. Humans get emotionally involved, and pride swells up in them, and they have sinful thoughts that lead to shameful, sinful behavior. Horses never do that. Horses don't lie, cheat, steal, gossip, and so forth. People do horses an injustice when they anthropomorphize them; it can cause humans to personalize the innocent things that horses do, and anger can result. When anger occupies the human mind, the person's actions often become regrettable.

Horses are super-sensitive creatures. If they already are dubious of a situation and are not "behaving" for whatever horse reason, then adding an angry human to the equation is not helpful. If anything, it makes a horse much more concerned about us at a time when we'd most want our horses to find comfort in us. We want to establish trust with our horses so that they will look to us during sticky circumstances and not feel like we are impulsive, abusive, inconsistent, untrustworthy louts who are just one more part of the problem they already are dealing with.

The Bible addresses anger in many places, but Ephesians 4:26 is very succinct:

> *"And, don't sin by letting anger control you."*

Sounds great, right? Just don't! So how does one not let anger control his actions?

By preparing the mind for action and exercising self-control.

I see this chapter's lead verse 1 Peter 1:13 in terms relating to both humans and horses. For the humans, we must prepare our minds to best help our horses. For our horses, we do well to get them, as Harry is fond of saying, "in the habit of letting go of a thought."

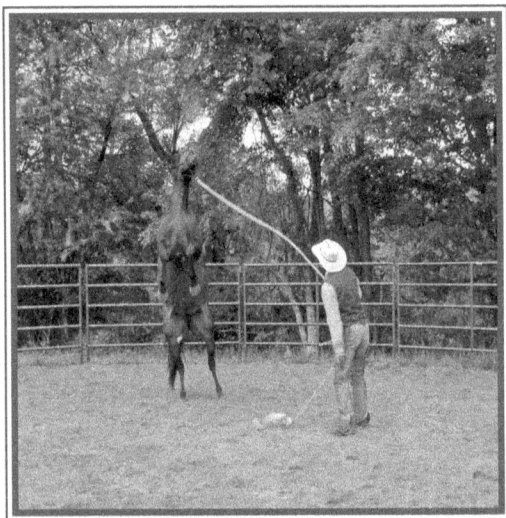

Mirage is stuck on a strong thought here, but it is nothing personal. I keep presenting my original request to help her find the sweet spot.

Later in the same session, Mirage has let go of her
strong thought and is following the feel I present
much more willingly.

Regarding the example of anger, once
a person is in a rage, it is difficult for him
or her to turn off the pulsating ire within.
A tape of whatever caused us to be angry
often plays over and over in our minds.
It can be very difficult to let go of that.
But we can work on our minds to be slow
to anger. When working with horses,
this is essential to becoming the kind of
horseman who can truly help a horse feel
better and "get with" a person.

So how do we train our minds to be slow to anger? Philippians 4:8 says:

"Fix your thoughts on what is true, and honorable, and right, and pure, and lovely, and admirable. Think about things that are excellent and worthy of praise."

Whatever our minds are filled with is what will spill out when we get bumped into. If we are occupying our minds with kind thoughts of things we love and a horse steps on our foot, we will likely have a very different reaction than if we had just been mentally playing the tape of how someone recently wronged us and we would love to see some justice meted out on him. Our minds, in this way, shape our actions and our world, and this is every bit as true in our relationships with our horses as it is with other humans.

Going to work with a horse can be a call to prayer. God tells us in 1 Peter

1:13, do something! We might, for example, develop a habit of praying to God to help us prepare our minds to best help our horses. It's an action that might spill over into other areas of our lives. Indeed, with me, many times my thoughts are fixed on something that went particularly well with my horse and that blessing and mindset go along with me into the rest of my day.

Now if we have prepared our human minds to work with our horse, how do we prepare our horse to "let go of a thought?" This was illustrated in the round pen example in the first chapter. The gelding had to let go of the thought of being over with his buddy to get his mind focused in the pen with me. That caused a profound change for the better in him that easily could be seen in how he slowed, how he turned towards me, how his head came down, and how he generally relaxed. If it becomes more of a habit to let go of those other thoughts when the human enters the scene and asks something of the horse, then the horse begins to trust the person and realize that there is something in it for him—peace.

I don't think the horse practices self-control in the way a person does. The horse is sinless and too in-the-moment for that. We practice self-control when we make a moral choice. We may over-ride an impulse that is of our sinful nature—don't lie, don't steal, and so on, all those things that cross the human mind. A horse doesn't have this dilemma. The horse is never in a moral dilemma. But it might be said that he practices self-control to some extent when he finds it within himself to let go of something else and focus on us willingly. But that is not the same thing as when a human chooses between doing right and doing wrong.

This chapter addresses anger quite a bit mainly because when I read 1 Peter

Breakfast in the barn during the 2014 Bible/
horsemanship clinic in Floyd, Virginia.

1:13, the part about "exercising self-control" speaks to me about anger. But, it needn't only relate to staving off anger. Self-control can be the act of stepping away from the things that our own selfish desires set before us to do that are not healthy choices. Self-control can be prioritising taking time to read scripture. It can be making sure your cup is full of true, lovely, admirable thoughts.

One thing is for sure...scripture clearly shows us that the foundation of the Christian life, a better life, is knowing the truth of God's Word.

"All Scripture is inspired by God and is useful to teach us what is true and to make us realize what is wrong in our lives. It corrects us when we are wrong and teaches us to do what is right. God uses it to prepare and equip His people to do every good work." 2 Timothy 3:16-17

Chapter Four

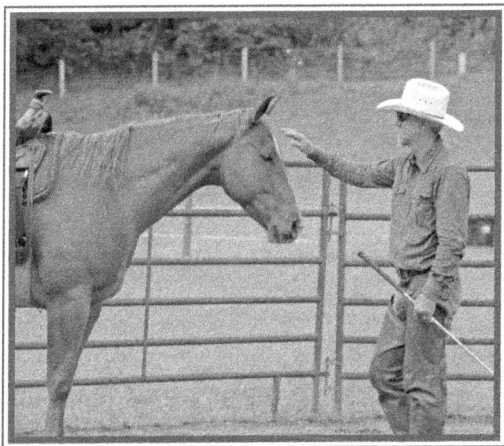

"Be still and know that I am God!"
Psalm 46:10

When can horses be still? If we reflect on the earlier round pen example, it is easy to establish that horses find it difficult to be still when they desire to be somewhere other than where they are. Our lives can be like this, too.

It is often thought that our modern age is busier than any other. We certainly do have more gadgets and gizmos to heighten our distractedness than at any time before. And yet, the Bible in Psalms provides us the directive to be still and know that He is God. This means that at the fundamental level, and regardless of the historical era, people are prone to displacing their minds off of God and onto their circumstances and onto other things.

So back to my question; when can horses be still? We have determined that they can be still when their minds are present with their bodies—that is to say, when they have let go of all the other thoughts that would cause them to be unstill. If we can convince them to let go of far-flung thoughts, like getting to a buddy back at the barn, and to focus on us when we are with them, and such experiences are positive, then they can find comfort, ease, and relaxation when they are with us and even become still. Horses can learn to trust us to take care of them and we can be capable leaders— ones who provide consistent direction, who set reasonable boundaries, and who generally operate in a manner that helps to provide peace and comfort to the horse.

When it comes to humans, it is faith in God and His Son Jesus Christ, and accepting the relationship He offers us as the all-knowing Lord who wishes the best for us and offers direction to us, that allows us to:

"...experience God's peace, which exceeds anything we can understand. His peace will guard your hearts and minds as you live in Christ Jesus." Philippians 4:7

(Yes, yet another scripture addressing our minds!)

I've joked on many occasions about how much time I've spent sitting by a round pen watching Harry do nothing in the course of my horsemanship education. The irony is in the truth of that statement. There can be plenty of action between Harry and horses, don't get me wrong. But many other horse folks I've seen (including other trainers and clinicians who are teaching horsemanship) are constantly driving horses around to make horses do things, like run around a round pen or get into a trailer. Conversely, Harry often sets things up for a horse to search for an answer (like thinking into a trailer or coming to him in a round pen) and then just waits awhile on a horse to arrive at some understanding in the horse's own time. I've seen Harry help some very busy horses become still.

With people, stillness likewise has

everything to do with realizing what already is there, set up by God for our benefit rather than by us adding anything new to the situation. After all, God has revealed himself abundantly in his creation.

"For ever since the world was created, people have seen the earth and sky. Through everything God made, they can clearly see His invisible qualities—His eternal power and divine nature. So they have no excuse for not knowing God."
Romans 1:20

If, as with horses, we humans let go of our preoccupied thoughts and just manage to be still awhile, we can realize what scripture reveals as truth: that God is God and that all around us He is revealing His splendor and that He runs the whole show. So, relax.

I can stand in the middle of a round pen with a horse who is ripping around the rail and be offering that he stop all that commotion and come to me, find rest, and feel a whole lot better. If I allow the horse the freedom to make choices, then it is up to the horse to see that invitation and act on it. We humans do possess the power and technology to force a horse to stop and stand still, but forcefully confining the horse does not foster the kind of relationship I am looking for with a horse.

The traditional "sacking out" method used by some when training a horse consists of snubbing a horse tight to a post and then forcing him to stand and take some scary object like a sack (thus the term "sacking out") being rubbed on his body. The result is often a horse who will stand when approached by scary things. But in order to achieve this, the horse has been forced to stand and endure an experience that he normally would flee from. That fearful desire to flee gets perverted into a shutdown mental state.

Often a horse who has been sacked out will stand stiff and wall eyed rather than flee when something scary is encountered. But then again, sometimes in this situation the dam breaks loose into a huge, undesirable reaction. The point is that the horse has no choice, and sacking out like this is neither a healthy situation nor a way to get relaxation into a horse.

A horse running out on the rail may not give up his romping around until I intervene with a bit of flagging or the slapping of a chap with the end of a rope, etc., to get him searching to try something different. But the whole time, at any point, he could stop and try being with me because my offer to do so is real, constant, and it exists even when the horse doesn't take me up on it.

See where this is going?

To me, one of the most difficult aspects to understand about God's dealing with humans is that He is All-knowing, All-powerful, and basically All-everything, and yet at the same time, He provides man free will. It wasn't until I got this horse analogy solidly in my mind that I really grasped a good chunk of it. I hope you find it helpful to see that allowing a horse to search and draw to us gives the horse the opportunity to choose to come to some important conclusions on his own.

As I am in the center of the round pen offering to the horse to quit running and come be with me, so too God is always there with each of us in this world. God is All-everything (as pointed out above). People denying that fact and running away from that reality do not change the truth of it even one ounce, just as a horse running around a round pen with his head turned outward and looking away from me does not change the fact that he and I both are in the round pen together.

When do we worry? We worry when we aren't sure we have what it takes to make things turn out okay. But we are forever inadequate to undertake the task of making everything okay and stopping our worrying. Our power is limited. The scope of our understanding and our ability to know what lies ahead are woefully insufficient in the grand scheme of things. The Bible is crystal clear on the subject of worry:

"So don't worry about these things, saying, 'What will we eat? What will we drink? What will we wear?' These things dominate the thoughts of unbelievers, but your Heavenly Father already knows all your needs. Seek the Kingdom of God above all else, and live righteously, and He will give you everything you need.

So don't worry about tomorrow, for tomorrow will bring its own worries. Today's trouble is enough for today."
Matthew 6:31-34

Which brings me to discuss an understanding I came to some years ago—one with profound implications in my life and in my understanding of horsemanship. It is one that I want to share, but it'll require its own chapter, so I'll get to that next.

But just to wrap things up with stillness and God's being All-everything...scripture tells us that there is nothing we can do to gain God's favor:

> **"Salvation is not a reward for the good things we have done, so none of us can boast about it." Ephesians 2:9**

That is about as clear and succinct as it gets. So, you need not, and indeed cannot, do anything to gain God's favor. On the contrary, He is in the round pen with us, drawing us, telling us that He already has sorted out everything we need. He not only has taken care of our daily needs, but He has taken care of the really big one—restoring our relationship with Him.

And this is the Good News:

"I passed on to you what was most important and what had also been passed on to me. Christ died for our sins, just as the Scriptures said. He was buried, and He was raised from the dead on the third day, just as the Scriptures said. He was seen by Peter and then by the Twelve. After that, He was seen by more than 500 of his followers at one time, most of whom are still alive, though some have died."
1 Corinthians 15:3-6

It is the very essence of the big mystery of life. We are all sinners:

"...we have already shown that all people, whether Jews or Gentiles, are under the power of sin." Romans 3:10

The wages of sin is death:

"For the wages of sin is death, but the free gift of God is eternal life through Christ Jesus our Lord." Romans 6:23

By our very own thoughts, emotions, and actions, we are condemned creatures who, made in God's image, are eternal beings and thus are condemned to eternal hell because of our rebellion. There is nothing we can do to solve our dilemma, but because of God's incredible mercy and love, God desires a right relationship with us. In fact, He created us to be in a relationship with Him:

"See how very much our Father loves us, for He calls us His children, and that is what we are! But the people who belong to this world don't recognize that we are God's children because they don't know Him." 1 John 3:1

So He sent His Son Jesus Christ as a perfect sacrifice for all the sins of the

world, for all time, who died on the cross
and was resurrected and lives now at the
right hand of God:

*"For you know that God paid a ransom to
save you from the empty life you inherited
from your ancestors. And it was not paid
with mere gold or silver, which lose their
value. It was the precious blood of Christ,
the sinless, spotless Lamb of God. God
chose Him as your ransom long before the
world began, but now in these last days He
has been revealed for your sake.
Through Christ you have come to trust in
God. And you have placed your faith and
hope in God because He raised Christ from
the dead and gave Him great glory."
1Peter 1:18-21*

That's what it's all about. Let us be
drawn to our Creator who desires to
have a relationship with us that we may
experience His peace that surpasses all
understanding because He has made

provisions for our salvation—because of what Jesus did, we can have a right relationship with Him for eternity in heaven if only we will come to Him.

Chapter Five

*"God made all sorts of wild animals,
livestock, and small animals, each able to
produce offspring of the same kind. And
God saw that it was good." Genesis 1:25*

At some point along the way in my horsemanship education, I was struck by the realization that the potential relationship and physical togetherness that can exist between a horse and a human already exists before either of the two come together and bear fruit. That is to say, we humans do not create any potential in the horse that equines do not previously possess before we go to fooling around with them. Or stated yet another way, as I am trying hard to share my thoughts on this clearly, God created the horse and the human, and within those two beings pre-exist the potential possibilities that can be realized between them; we merely discover what is there to be found.

This was a rather radical realization for me because before I became well acquainted with horses (and with the Lord, for that matter), I just assumed that any usefulness the horse provided for the human was the result of the human's big brain at work. I figured that the human molded the horse into a useful creature for mankind. This was coupled with the assumption that the horse had developed whatever helpful attributes he had, from the human's perspective, simply by chance. It was a somewhat seismic shift in thought to arrive at the understanding that—to use an analogy that is often discussed in the horsemanship circles I frequent—developing a relationship with a horse is rather like peeling back the layers of an onion.

Take the onion, for example. There is it. It exists. Man did not invent the onion, nor could man create one out of nothing or build one out of spare matter lying around. But—and this aspect isn't usually what people are talking about with the onion analogy, but I think about it—we can plant and harvest onions. We can fertilize and care for the soil where they grow, weed around them, ward off pests, and enhance the opportunities for

the onions in our care to do well. And—
to get to the part that people are typically
talking about—we can interact with an
onion. We can remove the husk to get
to the juicy inner layers...and with each
layer that is removed we come to the
next, deeper one. That is the point folks
want to make with the onion analogy,
that the layers exist one after another,
deeper and deeper, which is like the
layers that are there to be discovered in
our relationships with our horses.

Likewise, horses exist. Humans can't
create a horse out of nothing. Horses
have to come from previously existing
horses. Even if you think that one day
soon man will be clever enough to take
horse DNA and thus build a horse out
of spare elements lying around, he still
didn't develop the blueprint found in
that DNA, nor did man make the matter
to build the creature itself. These all
are pre-existing aspects of the world
we miraculously show up in and are

an integral part of. We can, however, nurture horses: provide them good feed, vet care, hoof care, and so on. But back to the relationship.

Begin by considering the physical relationship between horse and human. Look at how we fit onto them in such a way that the two creatures can act almost as one. Sure, there are other animals a person can sit atop, like a cow or a giraffe or an ostrich. But I think we will have trouble getting an elegant leg yield or lead change out of any other creature than an equine.

The same is true for the mental relationship between horses and humans. It is the communication that can occur between the two that allows for some amazing flow between the two creatures that again can put the two working together to the point of nearly becoming one combined/single entity. There is a special arrangement between our two species, and we didn't invent it.

While human interventions certainly have affected the various horse breeds over time, molding them to better serve our needs, like draft breeds for pulling and fast breeds for racing, it can not be rightly claimed that some symbiotic evolutionary dovetailing occurred over however many millennia to make the first equines and humans a reality—let alone all that can be achieved between the two species.

These are just my personal musing on these subjects, cowboy logic if you will (and I will get to my search of scripture to shed light on the subject in a minute), but if we use common sense, it is not hard to realize that statistically it is so far out there that some life-inspired slop decided to try being horse-like, and that little-by-little some other oozy stuff became more people-like, and that then some biped thought about riding some quadruped and that the relationship evolved together over cudzillions of years to produce a fine dressage horse or cow pony perfectly suited to the amazing feats that can be achieved between man and horse.

But putting my lay logic aside, I did some research on this to see what some bona fide researchers have to say, and there is a curious debate to report. In simple terms, the mainstream/scientific world doggedly teaches that species evolved over time—one bit of ooze developed arms and another fins, and they went on to branch out to make sharks and anteaters and so on. I find it very interesting that this is just an unproven assumption on the part of the mainstream, yet it is taught as fact and completely permeates the culture and defines the very foundation of the mainstream's world-view.

One of the beauties of God's Word is that we can and should put it to the test, explore its realities, and see for ourselves how it applies to our world. It stands up to study because it is the truth, so dig in. The Bible even warns us that the world is full of lies, and people are blinded by those lies, so we shouldn't be surprised by this kind of thing.

Basically, every science show on television and every science book in public school assumes the evolutionary position. However, scientific research has not shown even one single example of a new species evolving from another one. To be the very cornerstone of a widely accepted theory, it is fascinating to me that absolutely zero instances of a new species being created have been observed either in life or discovered in the fossil record.

Honestly, if this was a court case it would never even make it to court for complete lack of evidence. It's all speculation. And to top it off, according to some learned positions, science itself provides good arguments for quite the opposite of its spokespersons' staunch evolutionary ideas.

It seems that part of the problem with the idea of evolution is that it violates two of science's cornerstone laws of nature: the First and Second Laws of Thermodynamics. Law one says that the amount of energy and matter always stays the same no matter what changes occur to it (nuclear, chemical, or physical). In other words, nothing new is being created and nothing is being destroyed, although many changes and rearrangements to this stuff are occurring.

Law number two says that every change that occurs spontaneously and naturally tends to move from a state of order to a state of disorder, from complexity to simplicity, and from high energy states to lower ones. Evolution would require a general increase in order over extensive geological time, and/or the creation of new stuff, so this pretty much is a pickle for the evolutionists.

I like to bring it back to the relationship aspect though. Just think about it—would people attempting to ride dogs thereby create horses eventually? You know...coevolution (two species reciprocally affecting each other's evolution). Once it failed miserably for, say, a couple of hundred years, don't you think family after family of failed dog riders would give it up? Or how about riding cats? Would that make cats bigger and more horse-like to adapt to the situation they find themselves in or would it just infuriate generations of squashed cats?

I know the counter-argument might be something like, "Tom, now you're just being silly. We all know that the horse evolved by adapting his particular physical and mental idiosyncrasies to be suitable to his unique environment, and that those characteristics just happened to be the perfect fit for a human to hop on and get flying lead changes." To my mind, that's just way too far-fetched. The synchronicity that can exist between horse and human is just way too refinable to be a chance encounter.

What bearing does this have on horsemanship? If you are thinking, "Horse, I can make you do this—evolve!" it will affect how you approach a horse. On the other hoof, if you believe "Horse, we are made by God to do this together so let's see what He has provided us," then you are much more likely to peel back the relationship onion layers than to just force a horse to work mechanically for you. A person's view on this, it seems to me, can have a profound effect on his or her horsemanship.

I once saw a television show that had an interview with a fellow who gave an example that I often think about, and it comes to mind here. I searched, but I was unable to find who it was that came up with this, but I'm going to share it now as best I can and just thank him for it, whoever he is. This is such a powerful idea for me because it is visual and it provides a good way to tangibly consider the sort of gulf that exists between the likelihood of evolution versus that of God creating creatures. I'm no statistician, but I can grasp this.

Say you are from the northern hemisphere and you are traveling to South America. You fly down and then get a ride to your destination, a remote mountain village in the Andes. As the car approaches the outskirts of the town, you look off to the right and there on a mountainside laid out in rocks is clearly written, "Welcome to our town, horseman Tom Moates (or insert your name here)!"

Now what is your first impression? Do you think how amazing it is that these rocks formed in the earth and then surged this way and that way through thousands of years, reached the surface, tumbled around, and then arrived in that

exact position to spell out that greeting
for you, in excellent English, completely
by chance? Or do you think how kind
it is that your friends took the time to
go up there and spell out such a nice
greeting in rocks for you to see when you
arrive?

Of course, you immediately would
conclude that an intelligent creature with
the capability to move rocks and spell
did that bit. The random rock theory is
so absurd that you would not even begin
to consider it. And if someone told you
the random rock theory was the truth,
you would laugh and say that there is no
way you would take it seriously because
an intelligent person immediately sees
how completely implausible it is. And
yet, according to the fellow whose name I
regrettably can't remember, having rocks
naturally occur to spell out a greeting
like that on an Andean mountainside is
statistically way more likely to occur than
the complexities of life and all the species

just somehow falling into place without a Designer. That really makes me think, and I get his point. But anyway, back to horses....

To be honest, I think it is safe to say that there really aren't that many people who peel back and work with more than the first handful of layers of potential between horses and themselves. And don't get me wrong, even working with those outer layers of the horse-onion can be a wonderful experience and an amazing way to spend time and connect with an equine. But that doesn't change the fact that there are so many more deeper layers available in the horse for the human to connect with that could be accessed if the person has the knowledge, skills, and opportunity to get there. Working on horsemanship is the process of getting to these layers. These yet-to-be-accessed layers of potential in the horse and human for with-you-ness in their relationship don't exist there because of what humans or horses have done. They are a gift from God to be discovered, employed, and enjoyed.

So, after my above ruminations on the relationship between humans and horses, just what does scripture say that might give some insights on how to think about this matter?

"And evening passed and morning came, marking the fifth day.

Then God said, 'Let the earth produce every sort of animal, each producing offspring of the same kind—livestock, small animals that scurry along the ground, and wild animals.' And that is what happened. God made all sorts of wild animals, livestock, and small animals, each able to produce offspring of the same kind. And God saw that it was good.

Then God said, 'Let Us make human beings in Our image, to be like Us. They will reign over the fish in the sea, the birds in the sky, the livestock, all the wild animals on the earth, and the small animals that scurry along the ground.'

So God created human beings in His own image. In the image of God He created them; male and female He created them.

Then God blessed them and said, 'Be fruitful and multiply. Fill the earth and govern it. Reign over the fish in the sea, the birds in the sky, and all the animals that scurry along the ground.'

Then God said, 'Look! I have given you every seed-bearing plant throughout the earth and all the fruit trees for your food. And I have given every green plant as food for all the wild animals, the birds in the sky, and the small animals that scurry along the ground—everything that has life.' And that is what happened. Then God looked over all He had made,

and He saw that it was very good!"
Genesis 1:20-31

In the account of day five of creation provided in Genesis, God tells us in direct terms that He created "all sorts of livestock." Then, afterwards, He "created human beings in His own image." Also, related to our horse work, immediately after creating these beings God said, "... Fill the earth and govern it. Reign over... all the animals...." God tells us straight up that He created us and livestock (horses), so there is no ambiguity in God's Word about where we both come from.

If we then jump from the beginning of the Bible to the end, here's a fantastic clue about the role for which horses were created:

"Then I saw heaven opened, and behold, a white horse! The one sitting on it is called Faithful and True, and in righteousness He

judges and makes war. His eyes are like a flame of fire, and on His head are many diadems, and He has a name written that no one knows but Himself. He is clothed in a robe dipped in blood, and the name by which He is called is The Word of God. And the armies of heaven, arrayed in fine linen, white and pure, were following Him on white horses. From His mouth comes a sharp sword with which to strike down the nations, and He will rule them with a rod of iron. He will tread the winepress of the fury of the wrath of God the Almighty. On His robe and on His thigh He has a name written, King of kings and Lord of lords."
Revelation 19: 11-16

First of all, let me just point out that when heaven opens up for the second coming of Christ, the first thing that is seen (at least by John in his vision) is a horse! That is a hugely important fact to consider. In the Bible details are placed in scripture for a reason—they are for our consideration and our benefit.

Let me back up a tic...we know "The Word of God," "the King of kings and Lord of lords" is Jesus Christ. Notice that the horse is of such significance to the return of Christ that a horse is ridden by the Lord and leading the battle-charge pouring forth from Heaven. That only can be as God designed it. It is easy to conclude from this evidence that the creation of the creature whose job it is to carry the King (and His armies) back into this world over which He will reign is certainly not the work of chance.

It also is clear to see that when He returns it will not be as the Lamb of God as it was the first go-around,

> *"The next day John saw Jesus coming toward him and said, "Look! The Lamb of God who takes away the sin of the world!" John 1:29*

but as the One who "judges and makes

war." Since Jesus and the armies of heaven will ride horses, and God created horses and man, it is clear to see that scripture backs up the idea that the horse has been created by God to be ridden by man—and even has a vital role to play in one of the most monumental moments of all time, the second coming of Jesus Christ.

It also is interesting to consider that the above is not the first time scripture tells us that Jesus sat atop an equine.

"Jesus found a young donkey and rode on it, fulfilling the prophecy that said: 'Don't be afraid, people of Jerusalem. Look, your King is coming, riding on a donkey's colt.'" John 12 14-15

Perhaps this will provide an elevated status to the donkeys for those who think less of them than their equine cousins? Or perhaps it is fitting that Jesus, who took on human flesh, humbling

Himself to the point of being ridiculed, wrongfully accused, and crucified even in His innocence for our miserable sins, rides as our King into Jerusalem on one of the more humble of equines? But still, He is riding atop an equine. If you believe in God's plan for the world, then you must by these examples realize that Jesus's riding on equines is a part of that plan. If God created all things, then He created equines to play this role most specifically, and it is no evolutionary accident.

I found that this exploration of scripture fit well with what I was realizing as my work with horses progressed—that there exists within horses and humans special opportunities for relationship and activity, and that we can explore these and get to deeper and deeper layers of refinement in them.

It is a lesson for me to reflect on how unhandy I was with horses a decade and a half ago, and then compare that to how much more I am achieving with them today. And yet, I'm constantly discovering spots where I miss things, see them, improve in those areas with getting a horse more willing and relaxed, and then get humbled again by the challenges horses present to me. It is exciting for me to know that while I may never get to the bottom layer of all that God has put into a horse, I have an opportunity to go on and on with learning and finding new inspiration continually.

Chapter Six

*"The godly care for their animals,
but the wicked are always cruel."*
Proverbs 12:10

When we look to God's word for enlightenment, we know that God created the vast variety of animals, and it is His blueprint for each one that makes them exactly as they are. Furthermore, as we saw in the last chapter in reference to Genesis 1, we humans are commanded to reign over the creatures. In my mind, "reining over" means to care for and oversee—to be responsible for them— thus God places it firmly on us to put forth the effort to undertake the task of seeing to their wellbeing seriously.

King David in Psalm 8:6-8 echoes this obligation saying:

"You gave them (human beings) charge of everything You made, putting all things under their authority—the flocks and the herds and all the wild animals, the birds in the sky, the fish in the sea, and everything that swims the ocean currents."

There is a story I have heard Harry tell that comes to mind when I consider this chapter's lead verse, Proverbs 12:10. The verse brings up cruelty. Abuse is an act of cruelty, and Harry was interviewed by a reporter once who asked him a question about horse abuse.

Before forming an answer to whatever the question was, Harry stopped her and asked, "What do you mean by horse abuse?"

"You know...abuse," came the reply.

"Well, no, I'm not sure what you mean, exactly," he countered. "I need to know what you mean when you say 'horse abuse' before I can accurately comment."

This exchange spiraled downward as the reporter stammered and was unable to give a definition. She became frustrated and the interview died from natural causes. But a day or two later, she rang Harry back and asked, "Okay, so what is your definition of horse abuse?"

Harry replied, "Anytime we leave a horse feeling confused, he feels abused."

"Confusion" is in a bunch of Bible verses, both in the Old and New Testaments. Not surprisingly, the connotation of confusion is always bad. For example:

"It is a land as dark as midnight, a land of gloom and confusion, where even the light is dark as midnight." Job 10:22

"Your time of punishment is here, a time of confusion." Micah 7:4

"Some shouted one thing and some another. Since he couldn't find out the truth in all the uproar and confusion, he ordered that Paul be taken to the fortress." Acts 21:34

It is not difficult to see that, as Harry explained, to leave confusion in another when we could clear it up is to allow a negative impact on another. In fact, not just a small negative impact, but with language like "gloom and confusion," "punishment...a time of confusion," and "uproar and confusion," the Bible backs up Harry's statement that allowing confusion to persist can be an act of cruelty.

I might go a step further when considering this idea. If, as Harry said, leaving a horse feeling confused causes him to feel abused, then the inherent reality is that disorder inflicted upon horses by humans that creates confusion constitutes abuse.

Conversely, if "the godly care for their animals, but the wicked are always cruel," then those who are working to follow God's word will put forth every effort into bringing about order to their communication with horses to thus perpetuate peace and confidence in them rather than confusion.

That got a little wordy, but what an

important message. Consistency (order) in handling horses can help to produce peace in them. I have seen this to be profoundly true, at times, and even life saving.

I was called out to a farm one time to consult with a horse owner because he was so worried about a gelding being rogue and dangerous that he was considering putting the horse down. In fact, the horse had not had his hooves trimmed for a long time because of this dangerous behavior.

Now I'll be the first to admit that not every bad situation like this one will have the kind of outcome I'm about to explain—but in this instance, 15 minutes of working with that horse and I had a very gentle creature on the end of the lead rope. Before I knew it, I was picking up his feet and even put a quick trim on the front ones. The second time out I trimmed the backs. By the third session, I had him saddled and was riding the gelding (he had been ridden before, earlier in life). And to top it off, he was a real sweetheart.

At first when I worked with the gelding, he had tried all the nasty behavior in his repertoire with me, but I could tell right away that he was just posturing. He could have taken me out if he had wanted to, standing up on those hind legs and striking like a boxer in a heavyweight match. But he didn't. He was just working to get me to leave him alone. So, I got my flag and began to break through all that bluster.

I was very consistent with how I handled the flag. I would ask him with a little feel on the lead rope to go and circle me in one direction. When I got no response, I'd come in with the flag and make a ruckus with it against the ground off to my side until he began searching for what I was offering. When he showed me his belly button, I didn't let it worry me; I flagged bigger until he finally let go of all the junk, thought about what I was presenting, and went out on a circle around me.

It was amazing how quickly he fell in line with me. In no time, he was moving off the slightest feel on the lead rope, no flagging necessary. It was as if he said, "Thank you! I've been waiting for years to understand what somebody was saying so I could follow along."

This horse was rogue to the point of being put down not because of his nature—he was not out to get anybody. This was a horse who was so confused from inconsistent handling that he had learned to lash out at people to get them to leave him alone, and it had worked. I am sure he had tried to follow along with people in the beginning—he came through way too quickly with me for him not to have been trying before. But when the signals got too mixed up he found that when he reared, struck out, ran at them, and so forth, they left him alone.

But underneath all of that was a horse who really wanted to get along the whole time. People laid the ground work for this horse's bad behavior by bringing disorder and confusion to the relationship with him. But by changing that sad reality through proper communication and providing order to the relationship between us, it allowed peace to rule in this horse's mind.

It takes me back to chapter two and one of my favorite verses in the Bible:

"Don't copy the behavior and customs of this world, but let God transform you into a new person by changing the way you think." Romans 12:2

The mainstream variety of horsemanship this horse had experienced in the past had created confusion in his mind. That's not unlike all of us when we are being trained by worldly influences. But when God transforms us, he does so by changing the way we think. And that leads back to chapter four:

"...experience God's peace, which exceeds anything we can understand. His peace will guard your hearts and minds as you live in Christ Jesus." Philippians 4:7

Or, put rather succinctly:

"For God is not a God of disorder but of peace...." 1 Corinthians 14:33

Chapter Seven

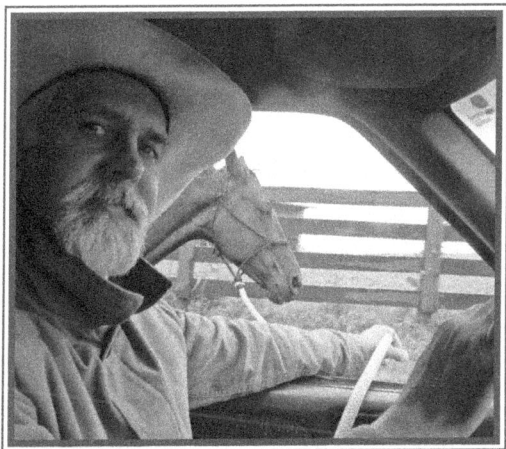

"Can all your worries add a single moment
to your life?" Matthew 6:27

I'm no ancient language linguist, but I do enjoy learning from folks who have studied the languages of early Bible manuscripts. Such insights can provide specifics about God's Word that our modern English translations don't articulate in quite the same way.

Recently I came across a translation tid-bit that sheds some light onto what scripture has to say about a main theme in this book—that, as Harry's quote says back in Chapter One, "When a horse's mind and his body are not in the same place at the same time, there's trouble in the household!"

My recent linguistic discovery is that in this chapter's opening verse the word used in the early Greek text for "worry" is *merimnao*. This is a compound word comprised of two words: *merizo*, that means "to divide," and *nous*, the word for "the mind." So a Biblical definition of worry is literally a "divided mind." Could there be a more perfect correlation to Harry's quote above?

Let's look a little more at worry. What does a horse look like who is interacting with a person and exhibiting worry? The head raises, the back hollows, the eyes widen, the tail swishes, the ears may flatten backwards...and as in our round pen example, horses sometimes will try to get their bodies to where their minds are focused by running around and even smashing their chests into gates or fences. These behaviors, and others that can stem from a horse's worry (like bucking!), are ones we would like to remedy if we want to enjoy an improved relationship with our horses. And surely we want to be the sweet spot in our horses' lives that brings about relaxation and good feelings rather than worry.

But there are other issues at stake beyond just wanting our horses to feel good and to perform properly for us. There are quite serious health risks to consider.

For example, horses can develop misshapen musculature due to being ridden with tension, such as a "snake neck." This is where the muscles of the neck bulge into an S shape from prolonged usage holding the neck high with the withers crammed down low due to tension.

Regarding that terrible posture, I have been part of an impromptu study at one of Harry's clinics. On the first day, we measured two rather worried horses at the withers when they entered the arena. After Harry did some ground work and rode them, they both showed significantly reduced tension, increased softness, a more level back, and more general straightness in their bodies. The results at the end of both sessions were that the horses were measurably taller at the shoulders by about an inch. There is no doubt that those horses' states of mind had a direct and observable influence on their postures.

Scripture says:

"A peaceful heart leads to a healthy body...." Proverbs 14:30

We know that a divided mind leads to worry. Worry wars against a peaceful heart and mind. (It is a mind at peace that leads to a peaceful heart.) So it is easy to establish that an undivided mind is one Biblical basis for a healthy body.

Another extreme physical issue that may be caused or exacerbated by horses carrying themselves "upside-down" (with the head and neck tensely elevated and a hollowed back) is "kissing spine." This is a very painful condition also referred to as "overriding dorsal spinous processes" or "spinous process impingement."

It is caused by the spinous processes (those sections of bone that attach to the top of the vertebrae from T1, the first thoracic vertebra, and run along the back to the hip to the last lumbar vertebra, L6) in some spots rubbing together. When the posture of a worried horse pulls the back downwards and the neck upwards, rather than being properly fanned out, the spinous processes can become jammed against one another and add to the potential for this problem. The pain from this condition can be chronic and debilitating for a horse. It is just one more example of why it is so very important to help horses be mentally focused and more relaxed when interacting with people.

Straightness is another place where a divided mind has an impact on a horse's health. Crookedness in a horse can show up, for instance, when a horse is not thinking about where the person is trying to get him to go. If a rider picks up a right rein and the horse steps to the right mechanically but is looking hard back to the left, thinking about going in the opposite direction, the

result is not straightness in that horse.
Rather the horse will have a discernable
crookedness in his body as his mind
desires to do something other than what
he knows he must do to avoid some
unpleasant pressure from the rider. This
is not with-you-ness, but the opposite of
it.

Looking further at a chronically
crooked horse, because of the
unbalanced posture, all four legs and feet
will not carry an even load. Over time
this can lead to a premature breaking
down of the limbs most used. Again,
we humans similarly can be very one-
sided and unbalanced in how we use our
bodies.

The list of health risks related to
stress and tension caused by worry goes
on and on. It is clear that a rigid body is
tight and suffers more impact and wear
and tear than one that is relaxed. Many
performance horses might have longer
careers and be better performers if they

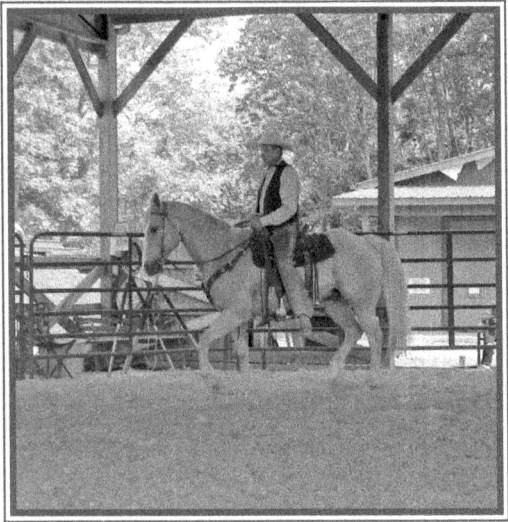

In Harry's intensive clinics, he rides five horses for four days straight. Here, at Mendin' Fences Farm in Rogersville, Tennessee, Harry rides a horse on Day One. Worry is clear to see in this horse with the elevated head and sunken back.

were able to feel relaxed and springy in their work—more like the way horses move and feel who are out being playful among a herd without humans around. And certainly some cases of ulcers and

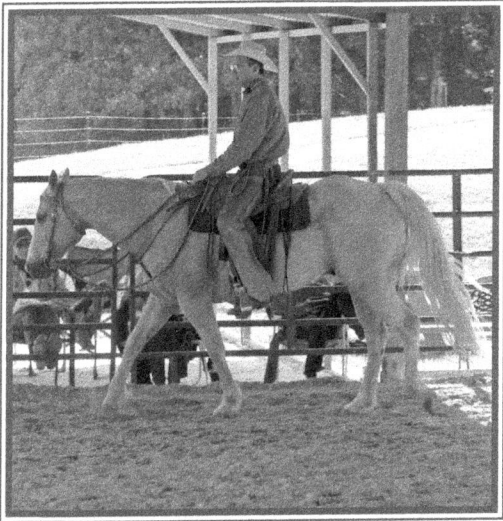

By Day Three, the positive changes in this horse are obvious. With increased relaxation from Harry's work, the horse's head is lower, his body looks longer, and the back now is elevated.

other chronic disorders are caused by the stress horses feel from situations where their minds are divided.

To answer Jesus's question in this chapter's verse, Matthew 6:27: no, all our worries can not add a single moment to our lives. But, conversely, worries with humans and horses can contribute to cutting lives short and chipping away at wellbeing, vitality, and serenity.

When looking at people and their worries, we have mountains of research linking heaps of health issues to worry and stress. Such troubles as high blood pressure, stomach conditions, migraines, and reportedly even blindness in some extreme cases has been linked to the stress of worry.

Jesus makes it clear in the Bible that He cares deeply about us and wants us to live healthy lives—as well as spend eternity with God the Father in heaven. That is why God goes to such great lengths to help people hear the Good News, come to have a relationship with and trust Jesus Christ, and understand how to live with peace of mind and heart.

We want the same for our horses in the sense that we would like them to put their trust in us and live healthy, vital lives. Jesus's question in Matthew 6:27 is rhetorical. He is pointing out the futility of worry for our benefit. It is a suggestion to recognize and give up the pointless practice of worry. How? The rest of what Jesus says in Matthew 6 speaks to that, and the answer is faith in God to meet all of our needs.

"And why worry about your clothing? Look at the lilies of the field and how they grow. They don't work or make their clothing, yet Solomon in all his glory was not dressed as beautifully as they are. And if God cares so wonderfully for wildflowers that are here today and thrown into the fire tomorrow, He will certainly care for you. Why do you have so little faith? So don't worry about these things, saying, 'What will we eat? What will we drink? What will we wear?' These things dominate the thoughts of unbelievers, but your Heavenly Father already knows

*all your needs. Seek the Kingdom of God
above all else, and live righteously, and He
will give you everything you need.
So don't worry about tomorrow, for
tomorrow will bring its own worries.
Today's trouble is enough for today."*
Matthew 6:28-34

* * *

Why do we provide all that we do for our horses? In some circumstances, horses provide a person a livelihood, although these days it is much more likely that horses are a substantial cost to a person rather than a moneymaker. No doubt many horse owners would answer simply that they love their horses.

All the time, effort, finances, and so forth are not something that can be used to buy a horse's affections—horses don't comprehend such quantifications. Thus, it seems people most often do what they do for horses just because they want to.

The horse hasn't really earned it; and sometimes quite the opposite is true if a horse's behavior looks more like a reason not to love them. But that's the thing... when we give freely to them just because we love them for who and what they are, we begin to have a glimpse into God's loving relationship to us.

None of us is sinless; we don't deserve a thing from God (unless it's punishment for our thoughts, words, attitudes, and actions), let alone a get-out-of-hell-free card.

> *"...there is no one who seeks God."*
> *Romans 3:11*

He loved us first and wants a relationship with us, and He wants us (actually commands us) not to worry because He's got all this under His command:

"Don't worry about anything."
Philippians 4:6

Worry in a horse is a massive blockage to our having the kind of relationship many of us are seeking with them: to have them be truly willing partners. But we can make a difference and help support horses to feel much better about doing things with humans, and the key to that is to get their minds with their bodies and get them focused with what is happening right there with us. Then the work of refining things with horses and peeling back those layers can take place, and a horse can experience increased relaxation about doing these things with us.

It seems that by telling us humans not to worry, God is saying we have a choice...that we can choose not to worry. If we did not have a choice, then Philippians 4:6 could not say, "Don't worry about anything."

And if, as the Greek indicates, "worry" is "split-mindedness," then the Bible is suggesting we ought to keep focused and be single-minded to avoid worry. If we focus on God and He takes care of the rest, then why should we worry? He and His grace (love and mercy—a gift with no strings attached) are sufficient.

"My grace is all you need. My power works best in weakness." 2 Corinthians 12:9

* * *

Unlike humans, horses do not have the ability to decide not to worry, but it remains clear enough to observe that a horse who centers his thought can become more relaxed. But, when we work with a horse and begin to get his mind drawing to be with us, we then can go a step further and send his thought (and then his body as well) elsewhere while maintaining a togetherness.

This may sound confusing at first, but I simply am saying that the horse can be directed to go, even at a distance from the person (or with the person atop his back), and perform a task while being mentally connected to the person. Stated yet another way, we can direct a horse's thought to do a task, and yet be connected by a feel to the horse because his mind is stayed on us to a certain level even as he performs it. And this is a profoundly good example of how we may go and do things and yet have our minds focused on God.

In the earlier round pen example we keep reflecting on, I drew the gelding's thought to me in the middle of the pen and he was able to relax and focus there with me. But soon when working with a horse like this, I will begin to direct his thoughts. I might ask him just to take a good look off to the right by offering a little feel on the halter rope in that direction. When he takes a peek, I release the ask and offer the sweet spot between us.

Next, I might get that look stronger and send it a bit farther away. And when this gets going well, I might put additional energy in my ask and see if the horse might take a step in that direction but then be able to bring his thought and himself right back to me. Eventually, I'd like to have the horse where I could send him with the lead rope or at liberty anywhere in that pen, at any speed, and he be mentally with me the whole time and ready to draw right back to me the moment I ask him to.

The horse can go and do things and yet be completely mindful of the human. There can be confidence and willingness in the person as a leader, and that can mean the horse need not worry when the two are accomplishing things together. Likewise, we can keep our thoughts on God—"on what is true, and honorable, and right, and pure, and lovely, and admirable, and excellent, and worthy of praise" (Philippians 4:8)—and follow His lead and let the worry go.

It may be easier said than done sometimes, but when you hit it right, as with asking a horse to focus here now, the results are fairly quick and can have a profound effect on how we experience what life throws at us.

Chapter Eight

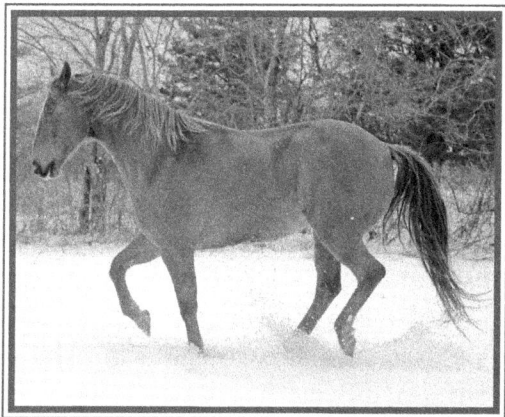

""Trust in the Lord with all your heart and do not lean on your own understanding. In all your ways acknowledge Him, and He will make your paths straight."
Proverbs 3:5-6

The opening verse above already has shown up a couple of times in this book. But I want to revisit it again because my big, handsome, sorrel Quarter Horse gelding Jubal provided me with a chance to consider it in a particular way back in April of 2018. It takes a little explaining, but it proved to be a great lesson when I made the connection to this verse.

This experience with Jubal was profound enough that afterwards I went home and wrote a bunch of notes about it. The challenge was to get Jubal to lope straight (that is, straight within his body, whether on a curve or a straight line). The project had been extensive and ongoing. In fact, many years ago Jubal taught me a good lesson in horse crookedness as he and I nearly trotted right into a huge tree. That predicament became the subject of the first chapter of my book *Between the Reins*. So you can see that the straightness/crookedness deal is a rather chronic issue with

Jubal, and it is one that has pushed the envelope of my horsemanship skills over the years.

In the winter and spring of 2017/2018 I was focusing on Jubal's going to the lope and all the anxiety that loping brought up as related to the crookedness in him. Even in the ground work, both on a lead line and at liberty, he struggled particularly with picking up the right lead. Going to the right, if he broke to the canter, which often required quite a bit of urging on my part, he most often hit the wrong (left) lead.

I could jump in here and talk about what I know of Jubal's earlier experiences before he came to me or provide a ton of details about this canter situation, but I'll keep the technical talk short to get to the point. Suffice it to say that Jubal more readily bends to the left than to the right, so finding the correct lead went much better when he circled counter-clockwise than clockwise. Asking him to lope in

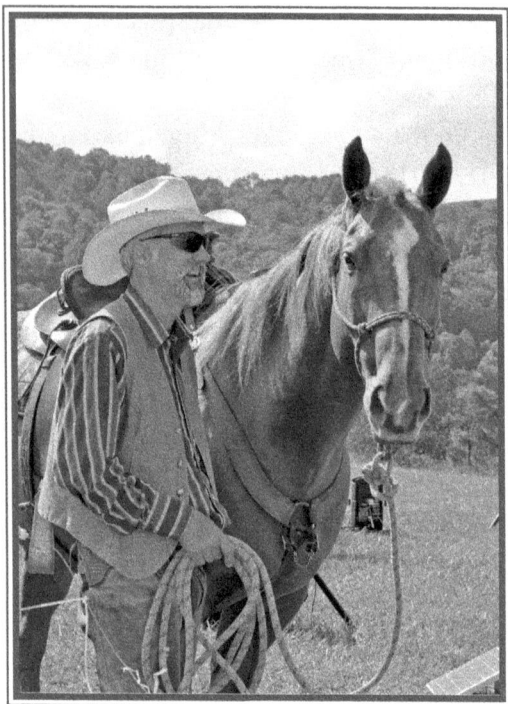

Jubal and me at the 2012 Floyd, Virginia Bible/
horsemanship clinic.

general, whether in the riding or the
groundwork, in a straight line or curved
path, was just a sorry looking mess, to

be honest. My heart went out to Jubal for feeling so pinched up about having interactions with people that his body suffered such crookedness.

I played around, working on this with Jubal for a couple of weeks. I put extensive effort into giving him well-timed releases for improvements, and that had some beneficial effects. (Horses learn from the releases we offer them—horses desire to be in balance with us and will get in the habit of hunting up the sweet spot we offer if we are consistent with how we handle asks and releases.) Yet, that old pattern still presented itself frequently. Jubal's worry and the physical results of it were deeply entrenched.

"I am leaving you with a gift—peace of mind and heart. And the peace I give is a gift the world cannot give. So don't be troubled or afraid." John 14:27

"Don't worry about anything; instead, pray about everything. Tell God what you need, and thank him for all He has done. Then you will experience God's peace, which exceeds anything we can understand. His peace will guard your hearts and minds as you live in Christ Jesus." Philippians 4:6-7

Now, if I was capable of convincing Jubal not to worry about anything, as God tells us not to worry in John 14:27 and Philippians 4:6 and many other places in the Bible, believe me, I would have done it a long time ago.

But notice where God in the Philippians passage says to, "instead, pray about everything." That is an instruction for us humans and a special opportunity we have to communicate with our Heavenly Father. As we covered back in Chapter Three, animals do not have the command of language as we do and are not capable of praying to God as we can. However, I would like for Jubal to experience increased security from our relationship, especially when we go to do something together. (And I pick up the slack and pray about this plenty for the both of us!)

The truth is that Jubal can experience some peaceful moments when I am around him, just hanging out. But the rub comes the second he knows I am asking something of him. That is where the tension starts building and affects his body and actions negatively.

"If we are afraid, it is for fear of punishment, and this shows that we have not fully experienced His perfect love. We love each other because He loved us first."
1 John 4:18-19

When Jubal and I are interacting together and he lets go of some of the tension about being worked and ridden, you can say it is because I first loved him. My love for him is why I spend the effort and time to try whatever I can to bring about a positive change in him so that we can do things together in a more relaxed and peaceful way. There is no other reason I would tackle this prolonged horse project if I did not deeply love this fellow creature. And believe me, Jubal would never come over, knock on my door, and ask me to come out and saddle him up. He would avoid that and the tension it brings up in him at every chance.

I long to see Jubal be the peaceful horse I know he could be around me when we do things together—and progress towards that goal is its own reward, and it brings me great joy. God explains that He wants that kind of reality for us with Him and that His love is explained in no uncertain terms in His Living Word. To think the Creator wants a relationship with me, and one where I am at peace moves me, too.

I have seen horses handled well,

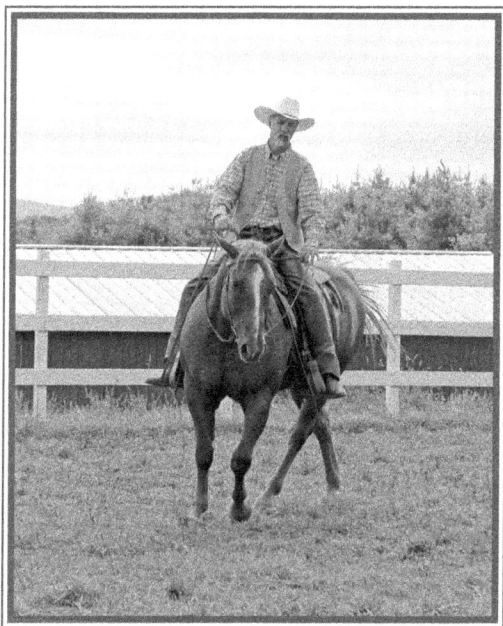

Jubal and me riding during the 2013 Floyd, Virginia Bible/horsemanship clinic.

and to varying degrees they let go of the kind of stuff that plagues Jubal. As a person, I have experienced the relief and peace of God when I have talked to Him about worrisome things in my life.

I won't lie and tell you that I have some utopic, worry-free existence now, but I will admit to praying often enough that sometimes I "come to" and realize I'm praying even as I'm in the process of it. That is to say, prayer has become very integral to helping me understand that what God offers is a personal relationship with people. The longer I go along in life with this habit of talking frequently to God, the more I realize prayer is about a relationship with Him, and it's a growing relationship.

It's typical that I'm praying before I get out of bed, when I'm doing chores, and you can bet I'm praying when I go to ride a colt or hear of someone who is having a struggle or am struggling myself. And it's not just the worrisome things I pray about. In fact, I think I actually may pray more thanking God for the wonderful and even rather mundane things in my life than about fixing the struggles. That frequent dialog with

God has really helped me to be more serene in general in my day-to-day life because it has shown me in many ways (answered prayers, a suddenly peaceful mind when before there was turmoil, and even positive changes in the lives of others to name a few) that God listens, is all powerful (Omni-everything), and has an active presence in my life and that of others as well.

With horses, if we don't ask things of them that we'd like to see (like cantering with relaxation), then we can't expect them to do them. If we don't talk to our Heavenly Father, then we can't realize that, yes, He is a personal God who answers prayers!

I used to worry (there's that word again, the one we aren't supposed to do) that I was bothering the Almighty with trivial things—things that I should handle on my own. But if we listen and believe God's Word, then it's back to Philippians 4:6:

"Don't worry about anything; instead, pray about everything. Tell God what you need, and thank Him for all He has done."

"Pray about everything," God says. "Everything" means every little, medium, and big thing. He doesn't say, "Only bother me when you have something really important to go over, okay?" And honestly, what is big to God anyway? Is there anything, no matter how big we think it is, that is a big problem for God? The little and the big to us are all kinda puny to an Eternal, Almighty, Omni-everything God, if you think about it.

So let's go back to my notes about working with Jubal. I live in the Blue Ridge Mountains of Virginia, and we have plenty of hillsides in our pastures. Jubal is kept on 20 acres that range from nice flat bottomland to steep hillsides. I was riding Jubal a bunch around that time. Mainly I had been working on getting him more relaxed at the walk and the trot before really getting into riding him at a canter. Finally, I felt like the riding work and his cantering in the groundwork was at a point where I ought to start asking for a canter from the saddle to see what we'd find.

One good use of the steep, grassy hills around here is that they are helpful for getting a horse to lope when riding. Horses seem to like to lope up inclines, so they tend to think about doing it themselves. Second, if Jubal lost his mind and wanted to tear off in the midst of the work, I hoped to be able to keep him pointed up hill and let him work against gravity so I'd be better able to manage the situation and get his brain back in a shorter distance than on a flat or downhill grade.

So I steered Jubal up a hillside and asked for a lope. The initial result was me atop as crooked a character as I'd ever ridden. He was so twisted in his body and all over the place rather than

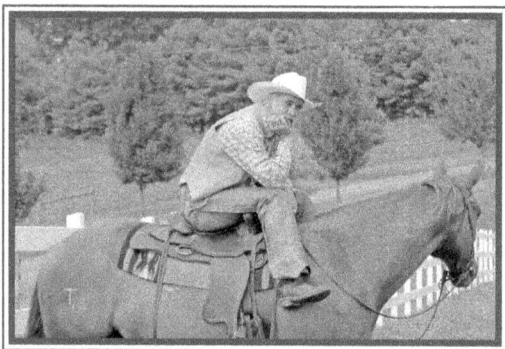

Jubal and me—a hard day at the office!

traveling straight with a feel like we were going someplace that it was like riding a snake. But I kept at it. Jubal and I played around with loping up hills over the course of a couple of days without much change.

On the third day, I did some ground work, threw a leg over him, and dinked around a little bit at first. Then I asked him to lope up the biggest hill in the main pasture. He trotted about two-thirds of the way up before he finally broke into that horrible, twisted excuse of a canter. Once up on top of the hill, I got him settled and I slid down out of the saddle. I hoped that dismounting up there would make it a more desirable spot for him to get to—that he might desire to lope up there to get me off his back (literally and figuratively).

These excursions up the hill had been heading in a direction away from his pasture mates Festus and Mirage and away from where we end a ride and de-tack. So historically, the top of the hill never had been a sweet spot that had provided a draw for Jubal.

I remounted and rode around a bit up on top of the hill, enjoying the broad view across a wide valley. Then we went down the hillside nearly to the bottom and loped back up it with the same crooked experience. At the top, I got off and gave him another break. I noticed his sides heaving as he began to breathe; with his tension, he'd been holding his breath during our riding.

Then I repeated the scenario again. Amazingly, on the third go up the hill, that horse took me straight as an arrow, loping all the way up. Jubal honestly blew me away! It was the most wonderful feeling after the terrible, junky stuff we'd been sorting through for days. I offered that he think about cantering up the hill, and off he loped, just like that. It was like a switch flipped in his brain, and he was between the reins and straight through his big body under me.

Words can't do justice to the wonderful feeling of that moment, but if I tried to use language to express the experience, I'd say things like "sublime," "magnificent," "awe-inspiring," "stirring"...no, they just can't cover how moving it was to feel everything with Jubal suddenly click into place after such a struggle.

After this ride I went home and made those notes I mentioned earlier to make sure I recorded this work with Jubal so that I could share about it in the future. As I wrapped up those notes that day, I concluded with a point that already was burning in my mind:

"This is much like our Christian walk, isn't it? When we don't have Jesus as our point up the hill to go straight towards, we get very crooked in our paths, our bodies, and our minds, too."

For this horseman, Jubal provided an excellent example of how crooked we can get within ourselves when our minds are not on the right destination. Chasing after what the world deems important makes for all kinds of crookedness in us. But having the Lord as our beacon and having the words and examples of Jesus as our spot at the top of the hill where we can find rest, our paths can be made straight. And as with Jubal, we can become straight through our bodies and actions as our minds become focused on the good destination that is offered to us by God.

When Jubal let go of his side-tracked thoughts that had him leaning on his own understanding and finally trusted in what I offered—and I proved to him I was trustworthy by providing a good place of rest and peace for him at the top of that hill—he acknowledged me, and his path became so straight that everything between us became seemingly effortless and in synch.

"Trust in the Lord with all your heart and do not lean on your own understanding. In all your ways acknowledge Him, and He will make your paths straight."
Proverbs 3:5-6

Chapter Nine

"Faith is the confidence that what we hope for will actually happen; it gives us assurance about things we cannot see."
Hebrews 11:1

Confidence is an essential ingredient to good horsemanship.

In the lessons and clinics I teach, it is quite common that a horse owner will struggle to get a horse to do something specific. It may be a task like asking the horse to rock back and step the front end over laterally to begin to circle the person during ground work. Yet, if I take the lead rope from the owner and ask for the same thing, often the horse steps right over with no hesitation. I can coach a horse owner to do exactly what I just did, mechanically speaking. But sometimes the horse just does not react to the owner as he does with me.

I have been on the other end of this deal, too. Plenty of times over the years I have struggled with a horse at a clinic only to have Harry step in and just line things right out. It can be supremely frustrating for both student and teacher.

The thing about trying to teach (and learn) how to overcome this kind of problem is that it involves "things we cannot see." Hebrews 11:1 speaks right to the heart of the matter, and I have come to believe that one reason for this situation can be the horse handler's lack of confidence.

If a person does not really believe that a horse will do what is being asked, then he or she is likely right!

When I go to ask something of a horse, especially something quite basic like stepping his front end over, I know I can get the horse to search out what I'm asking for and do it. I have built up the experience and understanding over time so that there is no question in my mind that I will be able to accomplish this with the horse and be able to build in the horse relaxation and willingness along with performing the task.

I can visualize the process before I ask anything of the horse. I already know inside myself what it feels like to offer the ask and what it feels like when

I offer the sweet spot when the horse searches out the correct answer to my request. If I hit a snag, so what? I will work with the horse until we make some progress. Full knowledge of all of this means that I am not the least bit worried about the outcome of the interaction. I have faith that what I hope for will happen.

But what does this important part of horsemanship look like? While we can see the results of confidence by how a horse reacts to a person, confidence is not necessarily something that we can see per se. Even in a person who performs confident-looking actions, if there is a lack of confidence regarding getting the horse to follow his lead, a horse can sense it.

As the often quoted and notable horseman Ray Hunt is recorded as saying, "The horse knows. He knows if you know. He also knows if you don't know."

Now, I won't pretend to know exactly
what Ray meant when he said that. But I
will say that I often reflect on that quote
when I come up against the issue of
confidence, and lack thereof, in people
when it comes to working with horses.
That quote comes to mind because
horses certainly do know when you
know. They know when you know where
their focus is. They know when you
know what you are asking them to do.
They know when you are confident that
what you are presenting to them is going
to work out great.

And they know when you don't
have these things working for you,
too. Horses are super sensitive,
intuitive creatures, and if a person is
lacking confidence, then even the best
mechanical presentation is not likely to
elicit trust and willingness from a horse.

Confidence is critical to a person's
Christian walk, as well. But it is not just
confidence itself, and not confidence in

the self, but confidence in God who is Omni-everything that makes the real difference.

Confidence in the Almighty God who means what He says and says what He means (as Ronnie often puts it) alters everything for us believers-in-Christ. It does so because it redefines completely how we view the very essence of the world, our place in it, and all of reality itself. To have confidence that God is in control of everything and is absolutely faithful liberates us and is the key to dropping all worry and finding that peace that surpasses all understanding. We can believe and trust that we are forgiven of our many and ongoing sins because God sent his one and only Son, Jesus Christ, to die on the cross as a one-time, all-encompassing, perfect sacrifice to atone for all sins forever.

One of the most impactful passages in the Bible for me has been John 19:30. It has stuck in the forefront of my mind

from the first time I read it. It is so
definite, simple, direct, and authoritative
that it goes right to the core of me. It is
a cornerstone of confidence in Christ
for me, too. It is Jesus's final words from
the cross, uttered the moment before he
died:

"It is finished!" John 19:30

This is another one of those
passages where I have come across some
information on the original Greek and
how it translates to modern English. The
word used in the original Greek text
for "it is finished" is *tetelestai*. That is
a term used in accounting that means
"paid in full." Jesus's last words as His
battered earthly body died on the cross
were declaring that the debt owed by all
people across all time to God for their
sins was at that very moment paid in full
for those who trust in Christ Jesus and
know Him personally.

For those who trust in Christ, your slate was wiped clean by His blood. And if it is finished, that means it *IS* finished. It already has been done. There is nothing more to do; nothing can be added to or subtracted from the deal. We live in an age where our debt of sin already has been paid. We merely have to accept the gift of God's grace. How hard can that be, right? Well, we sinful people do struggle with sin while we live in these earthly bodies, to be sure.

If we are confident in God and all He has done for us, then we will act accordingly. (Likewise, if the horse is confident in the person, then he will act accordingly.) It will affect all that we do. The Bible is full of advice for how to live a healthy, righteous life—but that is not a way to gain God's favor or to influence Him. It is, rather, the opposite. Living a Christ-like life is us willingly following God's lead after we accept His gift of grace, through faith, which means we are merely followers (disciples) of His guidance and are in no way proving our value.

He is in the round pen of our lives with us, offering that we follow His lead. He is handling the reins, and we can think along with His presentation on them. He may offer for us to be still, or to trot a circle, or to be haltered, or to be hitched to a plow...but whatever He has in mind for us at the moment, when we search for His will in our lives we discover there is a sweet spot waiting for us when we are with Him.

"You love Him even though you have never seen Him. Though you do not see Him now, you trust Him; and you rejoice with a glorious, inexpressible joy. The reward for trusting Him will be the salvation of your souls." 1 Peter 1:8-9

Afterword

One of the joys of working with horses for me is that onion aspect discussed early on in this book—that for every layer we peel back in our relationships with horses, we expose deeper layers to be examined, explored, and experienced...and hopefully we achieve ever increasing expertise.

With a better understanding and mastery of each layer as we dig deeper, our horsemanship improves and thus our relationships with horses benefit. It is supremely fulfilling to me when I help to bring about a positive change between a horse and me or to a horse and someone else I have coached.

God has provided possibilities so profound between horses and humans that a lifetime of study and good work on the human's part will never exhaust

all those layers. Studying God's word
is similar. One will never exhaust the
potential of the Bible to provide ongoing
insight into God's will for humans and
the relationship between Him and us;
after all, who can fathom God? The
Word is a bold spring from above to
quench the thirst of people in the dry,
dusty pasture of a sinful world below.
We can have faith that God's Word is
trustworthy. It is provided for us to learn
what knowledge God wants us to work
with in our lives.

And yet at the same time, the
message of the Bible is so very simple.
The Old and New Testaments point to
one main thing—that God will restore
man's fallen relationship with God. The
whole Bible, start to finish, is really about
Jesus Christ, God in the flesh.

As Jesus said on the cross before
taking His last breath, "It is finished!"
Jesus has paid our debt as the perfect
sacrifice for all sin, forever. In one way,

we need not overcomplicate that fact—
believe it and enjoy the freedom Christ
brings to life. In this world all people
will struggle between following the evil
that looks so enticing and is embraced by
the mainstream, and following the trail
less traveled...that which leads to eternal
life as is promised in God's Living Word.

I hope that by sharing some of
the Biblical insights I've gained from
working with horses, along with
my own musings on the scriptures,
horsemanship, and life, that this book
will help others find some new and
helpful thoughts on these matters.
Thoughts are what count. As with our
horses, whose sidetracked minds are at
the root of most of their problems with
people, so too our wandering thoughts
are at the root of our sinful ways and
troubles with our God and Creator.

So as I wrap this book up and
prepare to head out to check my horses
this morning, I'll just thank you for

considering what I've enjoyed jotting down here in *The Christian Horseman's Companion*, and certainly I'll give God the last word and leave you with one of those favorite verses of mine:

"Don't copy the behavior and customs of this world, but let God transform you into a new person by changing the way you think." Romans 12:2

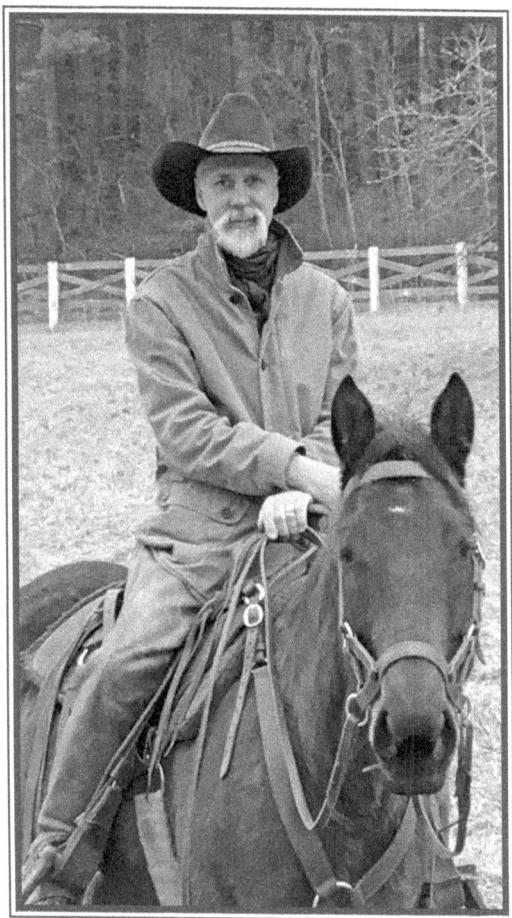

About the Author

Tom Moates is a leading equestrian journalist and author. This award winning writer is on the masthead of *Equus* magazine and his articles have run in many horse magazines in the U.S. and abroad including: *Eclectic Horseman*, *America's Horse*, and *Western Horseman*.

Moates's newest book, *The Christian Horseman's Companion*, joins his other 10 titles, including the five-book Honest Horsemanship Series, in the library of modern equestrian literature.

Moates lives on a solar powered farm with his wife Carol, a herd of horses, and a few dogs in the Blue Ridge Mountains of Virginia.

Book ordering info, Moates's latest publishing news, and how to contact him about horsemaship clinics and lessons are available at www.TomMoates.com.

Photo Credits